I Am This Boss B**ch

A Moving Self-Help to Empower, Embrace, and Accept the Female You Are

Stormi Paige

© Copyright 2022 - All rights reserved.

The content contained within this book may not be reproduced, duplicated or transmitted without direct written permission from the author or the publisher.

Under no circumstances will any blame or legal responsibility be held against the publisher, or author, for any damages, reparation, or monetary loss due to the information contained within this book, either directly or indirectly.

Legal Notice:

This book is copyright protected. It is only for personal use. You cannot amend, distribute, sell, use, quote or paraphrase any part, or the content within this book, without the consent of the author or publisher.

Disclaimer Notice:

Please note the information contained within this document is for educational and entertainment purposes only. All effort has been executed to present accurate, up to date, reliable, complete information. No warranties of any kind are declared or implied. Readers acknowledge that the author is not engaged in the rendering of legal, financial, medical or professional advice. The content within this book has been derived from various sources. Please consult a licensed professional before attempting any techniques outlined in this book.

By reading this document, the reader agrees that under no circumstances is the author responsible for any losses, direct or indirect, that are incurred as a result of the use of the information contained within this document, including, but not limited to, errors, omissions, or inaccuracies.

Table of Contents

INTRODUCTION 1

CHAPTER 1: WHERE'D THIS BITCH COME FROM, ANYWAY? ... 5

IF I HAD A DOLLAR FOR EVERY TIME SOMEONE CALLED ME A BITCH... .. 5
WE'RE WAY PASSED FEMALE DOG 7
SIT STILL, LOOK PRETTY 8
BITCH AMONG FRIENDS 9

CHAPTER 2: THE UNIVERSE IS A TRICKSY MINX 11

A DAY IN THE LIFE 12
WHEN IT RAINS, IT POURS 14
The Ugly Truth 16
CHERRY ON TOP 16

CHAPTER 3: SHE-HULK 23

IT ALL STARTS TO ADD UP 23
TIPPING POINT 26
The Rage Monster 27
BLUNT MEETS BEAUTIFUL 28

CHAPTER 4: DISASTER ZONE 31

EXPLOSION 32
IMPLOSION 33
STUCK 34
ROAD MAP 35

CHAPTER 5: WHERE THE SUN DON'T SHINE 39

THE EASY STUFF 39
If You Answered Mostly As and Cs... 41
Getting to Know You 53
THE HARD STUFF 53

    Let's Get Analytical *56*
  You're Already Enough 58
  You Are a Majestic Unicorn 60

CHAPTER 6: BURIED TREASURE 63

  Turning Self-Examination Into Self-Actualization 64
  Diamonds, Rubies, and Emeralds, Oh My! 67
  Things Don't Happen for a Reason 68

CHAPTER 7: AN INVISIBLE FORCE 73

  Fear Factor 74
  How Fear Is Strangling You 76
  Is This All in My Head? 78
  This Is Scary AF! 80

CHAPTER 8: MAKE FEAR YOUR BITCH 87

  What if You Weren't Afraid? 88
  What if You Were Still Afraid but Did It Anyway? 93
  Embrace the Real 95

CHAPTER 9: PEAS IN A POD 99

  One Is the Loneliest Number 100
    Your Mental Oasis *103*
    The Power of One *104*
  Family Knots 105
  #Relationshipgoals 107
  Posse 111
  Out of Office 113

CHAPTER 10: BACK OFF, BITCH! 115

  Exsqueeze Me? Baking Powder? 115
  Easier Said Than Done 117
  How to Build a Minefield 119
    Be Assertive *121*
    "No" Is Not a Bad Word *122*
    All the Options *123*
  Made by You, for You 124

CHAPTER 11: HATERS GONNA HATE 127

PRESSURE POINTS 127
RUNAWAY GUILT-TRIP TRAIN 128
BON VOYAGE, BITCH 130
TRIAGE 130
BETTER BITCH BRUNCH 132

CHAPTER 12: BOSS BITCH 135

BITCH, PLEASE 135
I'D LIKE A VENTI, ICED, SUGAR-FREE, PUMPKIN SPICE LATTE WITH OAK
MILK 137
I'M TOO HUNGOVER 138
POP QUIZ: WHO'S YOUR BITCH? 140
BOSS BITCH CLUB 141

CONCLUSION 143

REFERENCES 147

Introduction

Some might call me a bitch, but I wouldn't have it any other way. For me, being a "bitch" or having a boss bitch mentality, doesn't mean creating a scene in the grocery store because they're out of my favorite wine—even if I want to—or flipping people off in traffic—even when they deserve it. I'm not running around work letting people know *exactly* what I think of them or being difficult because I'm entitled to some sort of royalty status.

I'm not saying I have always been super classy and graceful with my boss bitch mindset or that it was easy to get to a place where I act from confidence and self-empowerment instead of fear. I've had moments that I will forever try to stop reliving because of the embarrassment I caused myself, my friends, or loved ones that always creates a little shame pebble in my stomach. Moments where my reaction may have, strictly speaking, been a bit much regardless of the catalyst.

For instance, my teenage boss bitch knew everything, obviously. Including when to "borrow" my mom's car in the middle of a snowstorm to go see this beautiful man who, at the time, was fulfilling *all* my needs. Not only did I inevitably get stuck, but I was also blocking his family in, which required having to call a tow truck, and I was sufficiently mortified.

Oh life, what a freaking shit storm. To weather it, we need more than meaningless platitudes about gratitude and messages of toxic positivity that are apparently telling us we've just been "choosing" the wrong feelings this whole time. Oh Instagram, why didn't I think of that before? You mean I could have woken up and decided I'm happy in my debilitating situation and practice gratitude for at least having a job even though I'm repeatedly harassed and demeaned on a daily basis? My bad.

No. What we do need is the power to embrace and accept who we already are as women, including anyone who identifies as such. However, that power needs to be conjured and cultivated by you to embrace your own boss bitch mentality and feel free to live your life unapologetically. Even though I have experienced challenging and heartbreaking periods in my life, there have also been amazing achievements through channeling my inner badass bitch.

By embracing who I am as a woman and understanding how I want to interact with the world, I have made my boss bitch my spirit animal and accomplished some incredible things that I would never have thought possible. Now look, when I say "incredible" I don't mean participating in Doctors Without Borders or summiting Everest.

Seriously, congratulations to you superhumans out there, but what I mean are incredible *real-life* moments that have added so much meaning to *my* life: raising my children on my own, realizing my family would provide a phenomenal support system, finding out what I'm passionate about, getting a PhD (which, by the way, also requires like 17 other degrees along the way), buying a home, maintaining that freaking home, and writing this book to empower and encourage others to channel their own boss bitch.

What about you? What things would fill in that sentence for your incredible life accomplishments? You have already lived through experiences that you can use to fuel your bitch fire; whether the outcome was positive or falls into the "that which doesn't kill us" category, these are the spark and kindling to our inner drive.

You clearly gravitated toward this book because it spoke to you—or to someone deep inside of you that's screaming for release. What do you need from this book? Who do you want to see in the mirror when you're finished?

That's a huge task, but I'm not about to let you walk down that dark alley alone. Doing this work is not all sunshine and rainbows; it's dusty attics and spider-filled basements; it's self-honesty and tears; but it's also self-discovery and confidence building. Lean into this book as you would a trusted friend and know whatever's going on, I've got your back.

You don't need anyone's permission to be who you are except your own. Bitch, let's do this!

Chapter 1:

Where'd This Bitch Come From, Anyway?

The word *bitch* gets tossed around quite a bit for so many different situations and associated feelings. Although used frequently and variously, there is an origin and progression to the term.

Before we can decide what the term means for us as individuals and how we'll use it in a self-empowering way, it's helpful to take a quick look at how *bitch* evolved to encompass women being assertive and how it's used for creating fear in our hearts over self-expression.

If I Had a Dollar for Every Time Someone Called Me a Bitch...

I'd be rich. Add in all the moments I've said it myself, and I'd probably be wealthy beyond my wildest dreams!

The meaning of the word *bitch* is incredibly interchangeable, from expressing anger and frustration to confusion and congratulations. In one instance, we're standing up for ourselves at work and in another, we're welcoming a friend.

I think some of my "favorite" moments of being called a bitch are when it's in response to assertively—and appropriately—sticking up for myself or loved ones, and my immediate thought is, *You think that was bitchy? You haven't seen anything yet!* Usually, that's accompanied with a slight smirk and a "hold my beer" mental shift.

However, there are also times when being called a bitch creates an overwhelming sense of sadness, frustration, and embarrassment. When it comes from a parent, partner, or child, it feels like you've let the world down. That can set off a downward spiral of insecurity and self-loathing that makes you question whether or not you're actually a "good" person—whatever that's supposed to mean.

But with friends, phrases like, "bitch, please," "this bitch," and "my bitches" are used like terms of endearment to provide levity and spark comradery. Among men, conversely, it's used as a way of being derogatory and to insult.

So of course, it's very confusing for us sometimes. We want to be strong, independent, in control, productive, and feel like a badass, but we're also concerned and scared about being aggressive, overly emotional, tearful, and labeled.

As if being a woman isn't complicated enough, we also have a frequently-used, singular word that casts both shadow and light. How are we supposed to figure out where we stand and whether the bitch we are—or are being called—is exactly what we're going for (basking in the light), or if it's derogatory and being used as an oppressive force (limiting shadows)?

We're Way Passed Female Dog

I'm a bitch; I'm a lover; I'm a child; I'm a mother; I'm a sinner; I'm a saint; And I do not feel ashamed. –Meredith Brooks

In her song, "Bitch," Meredith Brooks basically provides a long list of everything that she is as a woman, but everything that she encompasses seems to also fall under the term or be linked with the idea of being a bitch. So, you might fall under the label of *bitch*, but the term is so broad and includes multiple personalities of one person "all rolled into one" (Brooks, 1997).

I think it's general knowledge at this point that the word bitch originated to describe a female dog. However, somewhere along the way, the evolution of the term has broadened the scope, use, and intent. In the Merriam-Webster Dictionary (n.d.), bitch is additionally defined as "a malicious, spiteful, or overbearing woman; used as a generalized term of abuse and disparagement for women; something that is extremely difficult, objectionable, or unpleasant; complaint; spoil" (para 1).

When did we get from being used to describe the sex of animal to being used as a way to demean and control women specifically? Well apparently, this has been a thing since the 15th century and was first used as a derogatory term for a woman who was considered promiscuous but even worse than a prostitute— because at least *they* were entrepreneurs about the whole thing (Kleinman et al., 2009).

Sit Still, Look Pretty

I'm sure you've heard the term "Resting Bitch Face" (RBF), but if not, it's the idea that women have a "bitchy" look to their face when in a state of rest—not smiling, thinking about nothing specific, no flexed facial muscles of any kind. Some of us have naturally been given our RBF by sheer genetics, so regardless of the effort we may put into a first impression, the resulting assumption is "she's a bitch." I say this because I happen to fall into the category of "blessed" with RBF.

This can be very frustrating because I genuinely want to connect with people, which doesn't mean faking enjoyment, agreement, or placidity. Conversely, I also want people to know when I'm actually irritated, offended, and angry. Who wants their default mode to be RBF before they've even had a chance to speak?

This is one of those things that provides humor between friends, but can also make someone feel insulted and instantly experience the need to overcompensate with a disingenuous presentation.

Bitch Among Friends

All of that being said, the goal here is to find what being a boss bitch means to you personally and how to embrace that mentality without feeling guilty or apologetic. No, the term does not have a great history and is still massively used to inflict pain and control. But I want you to shed light on your inner self and embrace your seat of power.

For me, that's being a boss bitch. For you, maybe you call that strong person within something else, but the idea is the same. Your boss bitch is only for positivity, strength, awareness, self-protection, motivation, and support.

Girl, own your boss bitch! And with her, the beautiful being you have so miraculously created!

Chapter 2:

The Universe Is a Tricksy Minx

Ah yes, the universe and her absolute insistence on ruining everything. Do you ever just stop and wonder what she personally has against you? Do you spend time trying to figure out exactly what you must have done in this life or the last to royally piss her off? I mean, what other reason could there be for this clearly targeted, aggressive, and abusive behavior? I mean, damn! Pick on someone your own size for change!

The (sort of) funny thing is that this seems to apply to everyone. It's not that you're not special; no, quite the contrary, but it's more like the idea that the universe isn't actively discriminating against you specifically, just everyone in general, all the time.

But it definitely feels like as women we receive a disproportionate amount of shit, and some days, I have a hard time believing the universe doesn't have her thumb smooshed on my life. Karma is a real bitch and pretty much has a copyright for the message of "fuck around and find out."

A Day in the Life

The list of never-ending crap we are obligated to handle on a daily, monthly, yearly basis borders on insanity—literally it's enough to drive any person insane. The daily *norm*? What fucking asshole came up with that brilliant idea?

In a single day, at the very most basic level, you're supposed to clean, feed, and water yourself. It sounds easy enough, but it's not. Those items alone include things like grocery shopping, meal preparation, and time. I have to make a conscious choice every time I reach for my water instead of my coffee. Some days, some choices are harder to make than others.

Now factor in that there are a lot of us who take care of more than just ourselves, whether that's a partner, children, siblings, roommates, parents, or pets; all the living things in our life typically need support from us to grow and flourish. Daily.

Somewhere in there, while you're doing the important job of keeping yourself and everyone you love alive, you also have a million other things to do. There's the need to make money and that is usually both a time and energy black pit of despair. There are errands to run, bills to pay, sports to participate in, cupcakes to make (must be sure to include nut free, gluten free, dairy alternative, vegan options), plans with friends, plans to make plans, friends and family to stay in touch with, and on and on and on.

We're also supposed to "be healthy," making sure that the food we're eating isn't just empty calories and fits some kind of magical macro plan, and for some reason, although the above makes me feel out of breath just thinking about it, that's not sufficient exercise to keep your heart healthy. So, when is that supposed to happen?

It's no wonder the universe is targeting us; women are basically supreme beings of time and space so the bitch is jealous. Think about it: In a single day, you manage to wake up before the sunrise, shower, shave, moisturize, do your hair and makeup, make coffee, get dressed, make breakfast, get everyone else up and clean and fed, make your lunch, pack all the crap you might need in your day, drop children off at schools (maybe even multiple locations), probably get gas because you forgot yesterday, answer 45 text messages from your family, get to work and deal with all that shit—emails, phone calls, other people's emergencies—eat lunch, take healthy walking breaks so you don't lose your mind, drink all the water, but don't take too many bathroom breaks or it looks suspicious, be at your wits end until you have confirmation that the children made it home from school, stop at the grocery store or other errands after work, get in 60 minutes of exercise, call your sister or mom while making dinner, help with homework, feed everyone—again—do something relaxing and that falls into the "self-care" category, like read or journal or crochet, maybe watch an episode of some show that everyone is talking about, and then totally get eight hours of blissful, uninterrupted sleep.

Right. It's honestly pretty fucking amazing how much we're able to do in a day, but that doesn't mean it's easy. Quite the opposite. Especially considering that the rest of time is also plagued with chores like laundry, dishes, and other cleaning, maintenance on vehicles, the yard, and house, errands for all kinds of things, doctor visits and annual exams to follow up on, work projects, seasonal decorating, and tons of other random things that must be accomplished.

And just getting it done isn't good enough. We strive to be excellent in everything: amazing moms, loving partners, supportive friends, and high-achieving employees. But trying to be fabulous in all of the various roles we have creates pressure on ourselves and in turn, negative feedback loops of disaster.

When It Rains, It Pours

So when we have a little bump in the road, our feelings, emotions, and reactions are in such a frenzied state that it sets off a chain reaction. We're wound so freakin' tight that when one item on the list or activity for the day is disrupted, everything else seems to fall like dominos and we're constantly playing catch up for the rest of the day, week, or month.

Also, this sort of system creates a state of feeling like you're constantly in reactive mode; you're basically running around triaging your life and putting out fires rather than having the time to live in the moment, enjoy your life, and prepare for what's next. You're never just "out of milk;" it's never just one thing because everything is so intertwined.

Let's say you are actually out of milk. Well, no way that gets noticed until breakfast time so instead of easy peasy cereal, now *someone* needs to make toast and eggs. That sets the time table back a bit, and you run out the door without making lunch. Everyone is late. The kids get nasty tardy notes, you get another warning about being late to work which sets up a fun first half of the day. Lunch time, when you were going to run an errand, now requires you to buy food somewhere instead or maybe you can figure out a way to combine the two, but you had to park a half mile away from the building on account of being so late.

Now you have to hit up the grocery store after work and miss your window for exercise. When you get home, you realize you bought the wrong kind of milk and everyone's staring at you wondering why you're crying your eyes out with the refrigerator door open. "It's just milk, sweetheart," a loving partner might say, but no, it's not. It was the whole flippin' day.

Living from a place of reaction and defense, means that everything that goes wrong feels so personal.

The Ugly Truth

The out of milk example is just a basic way to illustrate what is going on for women during a day, but the reality is so much more involved and can include a wide range of inputs from irritating and inconvenient to serious and traumatic. The amount of random bullshit that has no business being on our schedules is enough to create very deep feelings of anger, hurt, and torment.

The ugly truth is that it's hard enough to function daily when everything is going "perfectly" so when we have to "start over" after trauma, heartbreak, disappointment, and other curve balls, it feels virtually impossible.

Cherry on Top

Aside from all the previously discussed items in this chapter, we also have to contend with our bodies, which are constantly changing and going through their own shit at every stage of our lives. You are constantly trying to keep all of your balls juggling while your body is wagging its own war in the background. I think sometimes we forget these changes are happening on a physiological level and don't factor them in as contributors to overall mental health state.

From a physiological standpoint, as we age our bodies are basically going nuts (*A Woman's Changing Body*, 2021):

- **Skin**: Although we spend a ton of time metaphorically "building a thick skin," we're actually doing that biologically as well. Until we're about 50, our skin thickness stays fairly constant, but then begins to thin, lose hydration and elasticity, providing fertile land for wrinkles. Not only is a skincare routine important from a "feel good" perspective, it's also essential to continually monitor for abnormalities, wear sunscreen, and keep that water pumping in.

- **Hair**: Women can start getting gray hair in their 30s and like our skin, our hair also thins out, slows down, and sheds.

- **Breasts**: These babies are all over the place. When they pop up in our young lives, it feels like everything changes. Well, there are technically a shit ton of things changing, but this one takes center stage. Then, every month corresponding with our menstrual cycle, they take on a life of their own and become incredibly uncomfortable. If and when you add pregnancy and nursing to your life, all bets are off with the erratic and painful experience of just trying to feed your baby. When we hit menopause, the breasts have decided they've had enough and begin to lose elasticity creating a sagging situation. Additionally, there is the real fear of breast cancer that needs to be screened for and monitored annually.

- **Bones**: Women are more susceptible to osteoporosis, so as we age, our bone density starts to decrease (around the age 35) increasing the risk for complications when we fall or bump into stuff. Also, as our bones become less sturdy and combined with some other aging effects, it can affect our height, causing us to get shorter.

- **Weight**: Does this need an explanation? Women can't stop being bombarded with thoughts and commentary around this item. "I wish I was as fat as the first time I thought I was fat," is a phrase a girlfriend of mine often utters, and it always makes me grin and nod. Women continue to gain weight for almost 10 years longer than men with a continual load from puberty through menopause. Excess (something that you and your doctor can determine for you specifically) body fat then contributes to many other health related problems.

- **Muscle**: There's a reason your "one trip" game diminishes, and you find yourself making more trips between the car and the kitchen. Not only does the creation of muscle cells decrease, but we also lose muscle as we age—about 10% between 30 and 50 (Corleone, 2022).

- **Sexual**: Our muscles related to sexual health go through all kinds of hell between childbirth and menopause. With the tendency for thinner and dryer skin as we age as well, sex becomes physically more challenging.

- **Digestion**: Where'd all this heartburn come from? Nothing makes me feel older than needing to reach for the antacids after every meal regardless of spice level or spending an increasing amount of time in the bathroom for every cup of coffee consumed. Everything related to digestion—acid reflux, constipation, taste bud awareness, bladder control—is in the process of slowing down as we age.

- **Brain**: Our nerve signals start slowing down which impairs our ability to pay attention, complete tasks, learn new things, remember where we put stuff, and process information (Corleone, 2022).

- **Sensory**: Our vision, hearing, and taste all become less optimal.

- **Heart**: Menopause robs the body of estrogen which is a natural cholesterol defense. With menopause starting on average between 45 and 55, we basically have an uphill battle for the second half of our lives.

Healthcare for women specifically can be difficult as our needs have been taboo to talk about with a doctor, and we've been made to feel embarrassed or ashamed with our changing bodies.

The advice from medical professionals to combat the physiological issues relating to aging include

- maintain a healthy body weight
- exercise regularly
- minimize alcohol consumption
- hormone replacement therapy
- exfoliate
- eat nutritiously
- get restful sleep
- drink plenty of water
- refrain from smoking
- regular checkups
- weight bearing exercise
- vitamin D
- calcium
- pelvic exercises

When, exactly, are you supposed to fit the above into your already crazy week? Even if you're someone operating at a high level with a well-oiled schedule that you can easily accomplish, you love your job, and have a supportive network of friends and family, with the above layered over your life, it makes the tasks and schedules we're used to accomplishing so much more difficult.

Chapter 3:

She-Hulk

It's really no wonder that considering what life throws at us, we inevitably lose our shit. Between what your daily demands require and your body physically making every day just a little bit harder than the last, sprinkle in some world input, and BAM! She-Hulk. Then you're left with everyone staring at you wondering, "Jeeze, what's her problem?"

Well buddy, right now, you're my problem. You're all my problem; did no one get the fucking memo?

It All Starts to Add Up

Just putting one foot in front of the other, keeping your head down, and surviving each day doesn't do you any favors. Although it may feel like you "made it" through, in the meantime, you're piling up stress and anxiety in your body and mind leading to an inevitable breaking point.

Stress on our minds and bodies causes heart health issues, sleep irregularities, reduction in comprehension and retention, intestinal problems, excess hormones running through our bodies, blood pressure problems, eating disorders, weight fluxuations, hyperawareness, anxiety, difficulties with mood control, headaches and migraines, body aches, more freaking heartburn, sexual issues, and excessive sweating. (I'm really curious to know what "excessive" here means because I'm sweating just thinking about it.)

Additionally, as women, it's a constant uphill battle against all things patriarchal:

- expectations to balance everything—work, home, school, children, partner, self (listed intentionally last because that's what we do, and it's one of the reasons we lose it)

- constant comparison, expectations, and bombardment from media—regular and social

- constant gaslighting—no, you are very much not crazy and are probably one of the sanest people you know

- in-your-face diet culture

- sexual assault and rape culture

- workplace inequalities

When we experience being overwhelmed, either for a short time or prolonged state, our brains will sometimes try to combat with triage techniques that may help in the moment but have overall harmful effects when used as a way for continued coping mechanisms.

These types of strategies only contribute to the pressure you're experiencing, even if they help alleviate negative feelings in the present:

- **Avoidance**: You avoid behaviors and tactics that are disagreeable, like nagging or making other people feel uncomfortable to prevent negative feelings toward yourself from others; you agree to internal and external compromises that are insufficient as a solution or self-damaging; you don't want to make a stink or draw attention to an already difficult situation; you end up going the long way around—literally and figuratively—to avoid certain people, places, or events; you drag your feet on making decisions or tackling stressful projects.

- **Disassociation**: Our brains are pretty amazing, but they can do some scary stuff. Psychiatric disorders aside, prolonged stress can prompt our brain to block the connections between things that have a negative cause and effect relationship to our mental state. When we dissociate, it's like having an out of body experience. This can also cause us to alter our personalities and identities to accommodate the needs of others. You may feel like you have no fucking idea who you even are any more and that's not "all in your head." (Well, technically, it is, but that doesn't make it any less of a real, terrifying, and depressive experience.)

- **Suppression**: This is the tactic of taking a situation or feeling, packaging it in a nice, little box, wrapping it in a beautiful bow, and stuffing it deep down into the recesses of your inner self with all the other little surprise packages that will explode like a jack-in-box once that wheel is cranked over that final time. These little packages of repressed feelings are quite fun at holidays, birthdays, and pretty much any gift-giving event.

- **Delusion**: I'm fine; things are fine; we're all fine; it's fine… sound familiar? There's a reason this is such a recurring and widely relatable meme. We'll envision our day, month, or year as a dumpster fire, but clench our teeth together, turn our back to the flames, throw on shades, and say, "I'm totally fine." Meanwhile, sirens are blaring, your body is trying to tell you to stop, drop, and roll, but you're not even going to watch it burn.

Tipping Point

Have you ever done an experiment to observe the surface tension strength of water? You fill up a glass all the way to the top, but not quite spilling over. Then you add a drop of water at a time to the glass. When you're eye level with the glass, you can see that as you add one drop at a time, eventually the water will create a dome-like shape across the top. Each new drop is absorbed into the existing water in the glass, and the dome slowly grows beyond what you would think possible for containment. At this point, the water is being held from spilling out by sheer force of its molecular bonds.

Know what it takes to break the tension and cause a spill? Just one more drop, and the surface tension breaks; anything that was "extra" over the top of the container's capacity is sloshed over the edge. One small drop, when you're already at your max tension strength, is all it takes to unleash a waterfall of emotions and reactions.

We inevitably use up that very last drop of nerve over something seemingly incredibly small, but the continual suppression of self eventually means there is very little left in our reserves to "go with the flow." So, even if that last drop doesn't quite create a spill, you would have an incredibly challenging time switching up the container or moving it to another spot.

The Rage Monster

Also known as the little, green-eyed she-devil that creeps out! This can be a monster that you deal with acutely or chronically. Your monster could come out of nowhere, lash out, and retreat to an inner cave to leave you to deal with the aftermath of the explosion, or they could be screaming, "I'm free! Huzzah! You'll never get me back in that cage!"

Blunt Meets Beautiful

Although these moments where we lose our shit or feel wildly out of control are sometimes ugly, terrifying, embarrassing, and shameful, they can also be insightful and honest. If we can take a moment to figure out what we're really saying when we're also screaming, discovering what our rage is trying to tell us, and understanding underlying emotions that come out as our She-Hulk, we have an opportunity to identify the beauty to our beast.

Well, at first glance, there doesn't seem to be anything beautiful about the situation or the feelings, but digging a little deeper to discover the "why" for the reaction will ultimately allow you to either embrace that part of yourself and give it what it needs or figure out what you want to change.

Or maybe you're totally fine with being a She-Hulk because that bitch gets things done and doesn't get hurt. As long as that's something you're embracing, and it's not a way to hide from intrapersonal turmoil, then in this instance, your beast is also your beauty.

I love the exchange between Bruce Banner and Steve Rogers from *The Avengers* when Rogers prompts Banner to become the Hulk, he responds with: "That's my secret, Captain: I'm always angry" (Whedon, 2012, 1:47:06). As women, I think this statement is more often true than not throughout the day. There's always rage simmering just below the surface and our task is to figure out what our own, best relationship with our inner—and outer—She-Hulk should be.

Personally, I love knowing she's there, right below the surface and ready to engage, but I've spent a lot of time developing our relationship, so I trust in the monster of my own creation. By getting to know this beast, I'm not afraid to let her loose and know that the situation calls for it.

Our She-Hulk is a beautiful design of our battle wounds that are meticulously woven back together, enveloping every piece of shit along the way, and fortifying our inner strength.

Chapter 4:

Disaster Zone

I think sometimes it might be best for someone to come by and section off my life with "caution tape" or "biohazard" warning signs. This would probably prevent more injuries to myself and others. Perhaps a sign that said "Caution: Flammable" or "Don't stick your fingers in the cage" would also work. I actually have a sticker that says, "I'm not a hot mess, I'm a spicy disaster," and I only need to find the perfect spot for it—like my forehead. I'm not usually one to advocate for face tattoos, but this might save everyone some time.

Have you ever seen photos or videos of locations after a disaster strikes? It's like all the signs of humanity and people's lives broken down into debris and a bunch of shit someone is going to have to clean up.

When we inevitably lose our shit and have an inner meltdown or violent eruption, it doesn't just end there.

Explosion

Your face is red, body is shaking with rage, heart rate is pumping, breathing is erratic, probably sweating, definitely swearing—and with zero benefits of actually exercising. The stress hormones released are going nuts, and your tears are on deck just waiting to release the kraken!

Probably the worst part of an explosive reaction to something is that there is collateral damage. This can take the form of verbal assaults or physical manifestations, but it's shrapnel that has been embedded in others (or through a window). Basically, there are now witnesses that need to be dealt with—er, I mean, people to apologize to.

Feelings have been hurt, words are out that can't be squeezed back into the toothpaste tube; the state of the union has been given, and it's looking like war is on the horizon. Your face is now on the wall at the grocery store or pharmacy or school pickup/drop off zone that apparently no one understands how to use except you.

Not only do you feel immediately guilty and a bit of shame, you also have to clean up your mess and apologize. This can be very difficult if you're actually not sorry, whatever was said during the "black out" period was incredibly hurtful, but also true, an apology won't fix it—sorry kids, you're taking the bus forever now—you were provoked, or you no longer even care enough to fix any damaged relationships.

And you know what, sometimes that's what you needed to do for the situation, you're fine with it (for reals, not in a dissociative, suppressive way), and there really is no aftermath that requires your attention or clean up. That's not what we're talking about here. We're talking about the times when your rage bursts out uncontrollably because you've been stuffing the hard crap way down. These are the situations where the reaction is not proportional to the catalyst.

Implosion

Not everyone deals with this mounting pressure and stress in an outward exhibition of their She-Hulk. Some people tend to do the opposite of an explosion and instead implode upon themself—but because we are the overachieving, badass people we are, why not do both?

Your body may have thrown itself on the grenade that is your rage, saving those around you, but ultimately causing internal hemorrhaging that kills you slowly. Everything comes to a grinding halt, and a serene yet dangerous catatonic state replaces your usual vibrant and lively self.

Although it's more difficult to visibly measure the aftermath, this is still an incredibly harmful state to realize. Your mind has shut down, circuits sufficiently overloaded, and a hard reset is in place to get back to the factory settings. No one should be going through the motions of their life, barely getting from one day to the next, and just because you're not screaming out loud, doesn't mean you don't need help!

The inward implosion causes strain on our cognitive abilities as well as increases the risk for developing or exacerbating other psychological disorders, like depression and anxiety. In this state, you've created a way for the world to pass by around you as if you're watching it on TV.

You may not need to apologize to anyone (*clears throat* except yourself), but you're clearly in need of self-care and love.

Stuck

The cyclical nature of this experience—build-up, explode/implode, guilt, shame, sadness—feels permanent and inescapable. Sometimes, we're really not sure how to describe what exactly we're going through and "just feel so stuck." Everything then feels like it's compounding to create an enduring situation: stuck in our jobs, homelife, routine, and relationships; we feel stuck with chores, demands, and errands; stuck with responsibilities, bills, and maintenance.

There's basically no breathing room to make any changes or even take the time to figure out how to start to get unstuck. Have you ever just sat quietly with a super heavy feeling of pressure with all the inputs and demands that need your attention with little to no desire to do any of the things you "need" to do and just let silent tears fall down your face while you feel the walls closing in around you with no way to escape?

The outside of you might be running a meeting at work, cooking dinner, helping with homework, running three miles, or doing the laundry, but the inside of you is curled up in the fetal position, sobering her eyes out, and wondering if this is what life just feels like all the time for everyone. It seems like this is just how it will be forever, and you're stuck. How could there possibly be any time within any given day to figure a way out of your perpetual shitshow?

Road Map

So, what is your body trying to tell you with its ridiculous behavior? It's not trying to say, "Hey, you're crazy; go check yourself into an institution already" or "Why, yes please, I'd love to do some jail time." Even though those seem like the clear and precise messages your body and subsequent behavior is telling you, it's much more likely that something else is going on:

- You have too much on your plate and there is literally not enough time that exists in reality to accomplish what you put on your list.

- The way you regularly behave outwardly is inconsistent with your inner, authentic self.

- You haven't invested any time in creating boundaries.

- You have deep rooted fear (including the fear of being labeled a "bitch") and behave in a way that above all else, keeps your perceived fears at bay.

- You cater to the needs of those around you first, and there is never enough time for self-care.

- The relationships you have are out of balance between give and take.

- You feel like there are parts of yourself you'd rather hide because they're "ugly" or "undesirable."

- You recognize the way you're treated as somehow "less than" by virtue of being a woman, and it makes you mad as hell, but you're also not sure what the fuck you're supposed to do about it.

- You're hungry—probably dehydrated too for good measure.

We've spent some time on all the "whys" for the reasons you feel the way you do and hopefully, at the very least, you feel less singular in your experiences. It's really not just you—it's all of us. I bet most people reading this would be nodding their heads along with you in solidarity.

I absolutely know what that feels like. And just because I've found a way to put out the dumpster fire and rewrite my shitshow, doesn't mean there still aren't moments that require silent, fetal position tears and doubts. The difference is, I know it's not permanent, and I have a map to lead me out of my dark labyrinth of self-entrapment.

A map is all you need, and that's what we're doing here together by finding your boss bitch mentality. The next sections will be geared toward building your own road map through self-examination, self-actualization, fear analysis, embracing the real, dissecting relationships, boundaries, and embracing the person you are, including your boss bitch.

I'm not gonna lie, this might sting a bit, but pop another cork (or strip another tea bag), take a deep breath, and be brave.

Chapter 5:

Where the Sun Don't Shine

I miss the phrase, "Why don't you go stick it where the sun don't shine." I mean, we have some creative and colorful things to work with presently, but this eloquent turn of a phrase just left so much up to the interpretation of the recipient. Either way, probably an unpleasant experience.

So, for us, where the sun don't shine means our inner, authentic self. It's possible you've buried her so deep that she thinks life is just a permanent state of darkness with shrieking eels waiting to snatch up what remains of her sanity.

Well, listen up buttercup, we have some shit to do, you and I.

The Easy Stuff

Yeah! We'll take it easy—especially if you just poured another glass of *something*, we should really ease into it to let the wine, or whatever, do its thing.

Alright, time for some self-examination—calm down, I said easy stuff first. This won't require too much deep thought, but will be a way to loosen up your brain juice to get comfortable with the uncomfortable that's coming. Think of it more like fun magazine quizzes you would take in something like *Young & Modern* or *Cosmopolitan* back in high school.

For the next few questions, don't overthink it. Seriously, don't. There are no wrong answers. Well, if I ask what's your favorite exercise and you say potato, that's not going to quite work in the grand scheme of the assignment, but good job for trying.

Grab something to write with and maybe a journal— possibly one of the ones you've been collecting that fall into the "too nice to write in" or "saving for something special" categories—and answer the following questions:

- What are your favorite and least favorite colors?

- What are your favorite and least favorite seasons?

- What is your favorite activity to do with friends/children/pets/your partner? (answer all that apply)

- What is your favorite activity to do alone?

- Do you prefer coffee or tea? (*Both* is a perfectly acceptable answer.)

- What's your favorite outfit?

- What is your favorite and least favorite meal/food?

- If you could travel anywhere in your state/country/world, where would you go? (answer all three)

- What is your favorite TV show or movie?

- What is your favorite book genre?

- If you had a dollar for every time [fill in the blank], you'd be a millionaire.

- If you had to live in outer space or underwater for a year, which would you choose?

- If you could have three super powers, what would they be?

- If you could have brunch with any three people (alive or dead) who would you choose?

See, that was fun and not too difficult.

If You Answered Mostly As and Cs...

Now that you have some answers about yourself to work with, let's take some time to tweeze out some meaning. This is the fun part where you get to think about the answers to the questions above, take them a step further, and relate the answer to other aspects about yourself and interests.

Unlike our old high school magazine quizzes, it's not a "mostly As" or "mostly Cs" sort of thing—we're not trying to figure out if our crush is as into us as we are with them. This will basically be a guided associative thought exercise, like a waterfall of connections, to help you dig a little deeper into the person you are.

Color

Any color or combination counts here; even the ones some may argue don't count in the true technical sense for the spectra of light, like black or white—we're not going to play the shade game.

For example, one of my favorite colors is green—all shades. On the surface, it's just my favorite color; I like to have clothing in green tones; I like designs, furniture, and artwork with touches and pops of green; I want (and I shall have) the green piece of any board game.

But when I stop and really think about why that's my favorite, it's more that the color reminds me of nature: plants, trees, moss, forests. Which also makes sense because I like earth tones in general. And when I think about that, I realize how much I enjoy natural beauty, whether that's inside from behind a window and bug screen or just taking a walk. It doesn't need to also mean I'm an extreme hiker or camper.

When I think about being in nature, I link that to feeling a gentle breeze or brisk wind, the sounds of forests, raindrops on leaves, outside critters, and the changing seasons. Those are thoughts I can link with feelings of energy but also relaxation.

So the waterfall association here is

1. Green

2. Plants

3. Nature

4. Nature sounds

5. Changing season

6. Energy/relaxation

One of my least favorite colors is neon pink—really any neon color, but pink works great for my example. An association waterfall in this instance, with a color I dislike, would look like this:

1. Neon pink

2. Flashbacks to elementary school

3. Pink highlighter

4. School was challenging growing up

5. Education is something I now deeply value and have pursued a PhD

6. Also an important value I ensured to instill in my children

So if you noticed, just because I started with a color I don't really like, doesn't mean it needs to have negative associations. With neon pink, I could have also gone down the Pepto-Bismol, hangover, late-night, bar signs, questionable decisions route, but I like the other waterfall better, and it speaks more to who I am now.

For each of the questions and answers, try to get an association depth of at least three or four; more is not only better but also more fun. When you do this, try to imagine it like layers of self-discovery.

Seasons

For seasons, you could find associations with temperature, clothing, types of foods, clouds, smells, sounds, different vibes, outdoor/indoor activities, holidays, vacations, gardening, and so on.

One of my favorite seasons is fall:

1. Fall

2. Spices

3. Baking

4. Holidays (Halloween and Thanksgiving)

5. Decorations

6. Time to be crafty and let my creative light shine

One of my least favorite seasons is winter:

1. Winter

2. Monotone landscape

3. Everything seems dead

4. Lower energy levels

5. Tend to hibernate

6. Lose touch with friends for a short time

Another reason these exercises are helpful is that the list can help you figure out things you might need to help balance out your life. For example, looking at my fall list, it might be good to try to plan some creative projects in the spring because that lifts my spirit and mind; while in the winter, I might want to make sure I invite friends over for a girls' night to bust some of the blues.

All of these types of exercises add up to being able to thoroughly answer the terrifying question: Why don't you tell me a little bit about yourself?

Activities

Associations for this answer can really help you determine what you value when it comes to your relationships, but also in terms of the kinds of activities that you enjoy so much, you also like to include someone special to you. These are the moments that really speak to the joy we find in others and the specific ways we like to reinforce bonds.

With my friends, a weekend getaway is my favorite thing to do because it allows for connection outside of who each person is within their families. Of course, there are still messages and contact, it's not about cutting people off, but the focus shifts from mom mode to who else you are and what else you enjoy. So, for an association, it's a weekend getaway, lightened responsibilities, crying from laughing so hard, crying from how hard life is, feeling refreshed and rejuvenated, and reinforcing bonds of friendship.

With my children, the true light of my life, I love watching them play baseball. In this, I think of being grateful for their health and abilities, skills they're developing for not only the spot, but also being on a team and making meaningful friendships, and appreciation for the drive, sacrifice, and dedication it takes from the whole family to support something that brings them, and me, joy.

Alone Time

When it's quiet and you have only yourself to entertain, what do you reach for? This could be books, crafts, painting, napping, exercising, baking, sitting in the dark in a quiet room, deep breathing, music, and so on. Think about what you pick as your favorite says about how you like to spend your time. What do you get from the activity?

If it's reading, that could be something like:

1. Reading

2. Comfy chair and blanket, feelings of being cozy

3. Mind is prevented from wandering as it's occupied but not focused on work, feels like a break

4. Curiosity and the suspension of belief, mind is engaged but in a different way than normal

5. Being surrounded by books is relaxing

6. Being carried away by a good book is a journey worth taking

Coffee/Tea

When did you start drinking coffee or tea? I associate coffee with my morning routine, job histories, and seasonal expectations. I associate tea with my family, reading, and health—seems like a cup of tea helps lessen the sting of many problems.

Outfit

Associations here could be weather, seasons, a specific memory or place, something special you saved for, magical jeans that fit you no matter what, event or other specific memorabilia, coziness, comfort, feeling like a badass, glamorous, holidays, and so on.

Meal/Food

Food is such a huge part of our lives that specific memories or types can hold very powerful associated feelings. Meals and food are also influenced by nature and time of year. I absolutely love my mom's baked spaghetti or fettuccine. So the association train that comes through with that answer is filled with family, full bellies, love, laughter, and light.

Travel

I love this question because everyone always wants to know where in the world you want to travel and that's definitely a fun thing to think about. But I bet there are also some great, local spots you love to go to that are guideposts for who you are. You may live near amazing national parks, vibrant cities, a smorgasbord of cuisine, an ocean, or three blocks down from an amazing bodega or taco truck.

What is it about these locations that draw your attention? I'd love to visit Ireland, but why there and not somewhere else? Think about it. For me, it's because of the luscious, green landscape, family heritage, to explore old castles, and my curiosity was piqued in high school when I did a report on the Irish Potato Famine.

What's On?

Associations for this question could be the feelings you experience from watching—humor, romance, drama, sadness, thrilling, scary. Why do you like that? Do you have a serious day and just love to sit and watch some mindless humor or reality shows? Or do you relax watching other people deal with drama that's way crazier than yours and keep track of their ranch fortunes? Who are you watching with? What do you both get from this routine?

Book Genre

I read a couple of genres consistently, but I will often throw in others when I feel in the mood for something different. Think about what books you gravitate toward and why. What is it about that topic that holds your attention or is able to be transportive? Maybe if you constantly reach for fantasy or science fiction, you're looking for things not of this reality to escape with your mind; if you reach for more hard-hitting, make-you-ugly-cry, contemporary, maybe you really enjoy feeling something meaningful and connecting with people through the pages.

If I Had a Dollar

My word here is definitely *Mom*. My children are my light and although *Mom* is not always accompanied with graciousness or patience (most of the time it is), knowing this word would make me a theoretical millionaire warms my heart. My association for this question would include feeling proud of my accomplishments, as well as my trials, but also so much pride in my children seeing every ounce of effort I put in reflected in their hearts and souls.

Of course, the word *bitch* also fits this question, but that association waterfall would include things like power, accountability, knowledge, and self-examination. If I had done this exercise early on, it would probably be more hurtful or shameful associations, but self-examination—asking questions like, "What was it that elicited such a remark?"—has helped me understand that the real bitch of the situation is the other person bitching about being stood up to, not being allowed to take advantage, being caught in a lie, upset with being disagreed with, or outmaneuvered.

Outer Space/Underwater

Both of these answers explore the idea of the unknown and what kinds of things are curious to you. Are you more curious about what actually exists within our planet, living undisturbed, and the amazing, underwater world of bioluminescence? Or does your mind stretch out into the recesses of space and wonder if there are other forms of life who also think the universe is a trying bitch?

If you prefer underwater, is it because being in a cold, submerged, windowed space makes you feel calm or flying—floating—on a spaceship gives you a feeling of weightlessness and release?

Superpowers

Maybe you have a standard answer already locked and loaded for this, but take a minute to think more about why these over others? If it's something like invisibility, is it because you already feel the need to shy away into the background or do you really just enjoy juicy gossip and would love to be a fly on the wall for any conversation?

My picks would be to read minds, increase or decrease the speed of time, and mood elevator—for those stubborn assholes we run into from time to time. "Hey! Cheer up fucker!" might do the trick as well.

The desire to read minds for me, comes from a deep desire to empower, support, and encourage others, especially people who have a hard time expressing themselves. There are, of course, other benefits like knowing when people aren't being truthful or what they really think about you. But honestly, I'd rather know so I could spend my precious time with people who are genuine and authentic.

A mind reading ability would have come in extremely handy when my children were babies and only 19 months apart. Whatever parts of my mind are lost to insanity, it has to be from that period of time as a young mother just trying to figure out how to keep those two precious humans, and myself, alive.

Brunch Besties

This one is pretty important because it forces you to recognize what it is in others that you deeply value or want to emulate. The idea of three people is just a minimum; feel free to invite everyone to the brunch who you look up to or wish was still around to share some wisdom, memories, and bubbles.

My table would be filled with one of my best friends who passed away a few years ago, my grandmother, my other best friend, and my mom, but also Kristen Green, Oprah, and Susan Wojcicki—all women who have and continue to make huge impacts and empower others. In the people I admire, I clearly identify with the desire to empower and impact but also the strength of friendship and familiar bonds.

I'm not sure if this brunch would be more laughing or crying, but it would be a fucking good time.

Getting to Know You

After going through that exercise, you should have some solid ideas about what drives your curiosity and supports your motivation. You may even have a better understanding of why you feel specific ways about certain situations or times of the year.

No matter what, that was just a few fun questions, and you now have a lot to work with as well as a model if you want to get to know yourself better. You should also take away that your desires and passions run *deep*; there is a lot going on inside you, even if you feel numb to the world. Your above answers and association waterfalls are just the tip of the iceberg as to what makes up the person you are.

The Hard Stuff

Alight. Deep breath. Even though it was the fun and "easy" stuff, that was still quite a bit of deep diving into how you think about who you are. We're not stopping there—you have a boss bitch buried inside of you, and we're going to find her and set her free.

Eeek! I know it's scary; the questions here will be deeper and sometimes difficult to answer because sometimes being honest with ourselves is the hardest thing in the world. Although we want to be honest, we don't want to judge, blame, or berate ourselves for the answers. So, try to be mindful with your self-talk as you work on self-examination.

Grab your snazzy notebook again and thoughtfully answer the following questions:

- When (times of day, year, with different people, various events, locations, work, home, etc.) do you experience moments of the following emotions:

    - happiness
    - love
    - contentment
    - pleasure
    - empowerment
    - inspiration
    - boldness
    - unique

- refreshed
- amusement

• When do you experience moments of the following emotions:

- sadness
- anger
- frustration
- resentment
- doubt
- agitation
- rage
- embarrassment
- hesitation
- depression

• What kinds of situations, actions, and accomplishments make you feel fulfilled?

• When or in what areas of your life do you feel unfulfilled?

- When do your actions differ from your emotions?

    - How would you react differently if there weren't possible negative or uncomfortable consequences?

- Do you feel balanced emotionally, mentally, and physically?

    - Are there any areas of your life that overshadow the others?

    - What types of feelings, people, or situations cause you to feel unbalanced?

- If you think of your life made up of pie wedges, how many different wedges are you trying to cut your pie into?

    - What pieces are bigger than others in terms of demand on time and energy?

    - What pieces do you wish you could spend more time with?

- If you could travel back in time 1–5 years ago and give yourself advice, what would it be?

Let's Get Analytical

The answers to the hard questions lend themselves to being fairly clear in terms of "what does this mean." It's really what makes them difficult in the first place. When you're analyzing what you've answered above, the real trick is self-honesty. But it's one thing to know these things and quite another to see them written down and "exposed."

When you're working on self-examination and carving out your authenticity, it's really easy to be critical. Give yourself as much grace and patience as you do with others, which I'm sure is a lot.

The other thing to look for when you're reviewing your responses to the above are patterns that you can trace back to specific people, locations, or situations. If something continually comes up more than others, that would be a great place to start that would have the most impact.

That, however, can also be a scary place to start so if it's too much at the moment, pick something else! You cannot get it wrong; the only thing you shouldn't do is ignore your genuine feelings and stuff this shit back deep down.

Also, within the above list of questions are things that bring you joy, satisfaction, and contentment. Don't overlook the power of those feelings and try to increase those situations within your daily life as much as possible.

You're Already Enough

It's very difficult to look at your life through a critical, but at the same time unapologetic, lens. Unless I'm totally out of the loop, I'm pretty sure time travel isn't a thing (yet, but God help some fools in my past if it ever becomes possible) so it's a waste of time, effort, and tears to dwell on what you should've, could've done differently.

I'm not saying hold it in. Let those tears flow. They're good for your skin and cleanse your tear ducts (this falls under the "things I tell myself to make me feel better about it" category). No shame in crying but don't lose yourself down a rabbit hole of regret.

You are who you are now. Period. But everything that you've gone through, all the decisions you've made—good, bad, and ugly—have created a person with a unique set of skills—Liam Neilson style skills from *Taken* if you'd like to think of like that: "But what I do have are a very particular set of skills, skills I have acquired over a very long career, skills that make me a nightmare for people like you" (Morel, 2008, 28:32).

There is no need to change who you are unless you are unhappy with the person you present to the world. However, if that's the case, it's probably more of a situation where how you act is disingenuous with who you actually are. You are already able to embrace what's inside of you and use that as a strong foundation to build upon.

There are things about you that people love and these are clues to help you discover the person you are. Sometimes it really only takes opening our ears and really *listening*, not just hearing, what other people are telling us.

One of my friends, let's call her Lizzy, is a very strong-willed and vocal advocate for doing the right thing. At work, however, that sometimes landed her with the "bitch" label, and it's something she's terribly self-conscious about. Additionally, her crazy and chaotic life makes her seem flaky and perpetually late. She is self-critical of these things and sees herself as a "bad friend" who is unreliable and quick to temper.

Those things couldn't be further from the truth! Lizzy is one of the most dependable people I have ever known with the biggest, kindest heart in the world, and would bend over backward to help someone in need. Even when I tell her these things, she's not listening because she can't see past her perceived reputation.

Think about that for a minute and answer the following question:

- What is it about you that people are already drawn to?

- What compliments do you receive from your friends, family, coworkers, or even strangers?

- If your best friend was sitting with you right now, what would they say were your very best qualities?

It is also totally okay to want to be different or change some behaviors to better align with who you want to be if there is a discrepancy between who you are and who you wish you could be. We aren't cast in stone, even though it feels like it, and can decide on any day, in any moment, to change our narrative.

There is literally nothing else that exists except from this day forward. What you already carry is part of your strength; you're basically an Olympic bodybuilder at this point, so use your core to powerlift your ass out of the darkness.

You Are a Majestic Unicorn

My strength does not look like yours. I haven't lived your life, nor you mine. I would not want to be trapped on an island with a bunch of copies of myself—sure, we might agree on all the rules for society, but I don't know how to make fire from sticks alone, so we're all basically fucked.

The point is, not only is it a good thing to be unique but necessary for the survival of humanity as a whole. That's literally how evolution works—it's the mutations that save us all. So, mutations and abnormalities are actually essential for change and growth. These things do not need to have negative connotations; they are the result of living through adversity and coming out the other side due your unique adaptations.

When the lovely bitch of a universe throws asteroids at us, it's our unique blend of skills and intuition that coalesce to provide resistance, persistence, strength, and counterattack.

Chapter 6:

Buried Treasure

So you see, you have a wealth of buried treasure hidden inside you. On your dive deep into the recesses of self, finding those nuggets is not simply about locating them. From their time at the bottom of the ocean, they probably look more like crustaceans rather than the sparkling gems that they are and could easily be discarded or mistaken for trash.

As we go through our days on autopilot, it's natural to maintain looking outward only: It's easy, comfortable, and allows us to just keep putting one foot in front of the other.

But that doesn't necessarily make us happy or fully realized human beings who embrace their inner boss bitch. Somewhere deep inside a sense of disjointedness takes over, making us feel like Frankenstein's monster—talk about a study in self-loathing and deep insight into the actualization of self!

Turning Self-Examination Into Self-Actualization

When you take self-examination and transition to self-actualization, you are taking those crusty looking shit rocks, chiseling away at the shell, and polishing what's inside into shining, precious, extremely valuable gems.

So, what exactly is the difference between self-examination and self-actualization? The examination part is what you've done a little bit of in the previous chapter by identifying some of your core beliefs, feelings, thoughts, and passions. Great, you have a list, so what?

Actualization comes when you fully embrace, utilize, highlight, admire, cultivate, and share those integral fibers of your being. It's like taking your emerald, throwing on some spit shine, and displaying it in an interest-bearing account. In other words, when you take your treasures and make them work for you, your personal value and self-worth increases as well.

With the information you have about yourself from Chapter 5, pick one or two things to work on moving from examination over to actualization. I don't care if you pick easy or hard stuff; this is your journey, so it's more important to pick something you know you'll have the highest probability of accomplishing. If you realized that you're drawn to a cozy vibe and that really ignites feelings of happiness, spend some time transforming chaotic and stressful areas (like perhaps a work desk or office) into a space that aligns with a cozy message.

If you discover that you tend to feel more depressed when you go for long periods of time between talking with friends and family, make a schedule to ensure you're reaching out regularly or have standing plans to have a chitchat.

Perhaps when you drew out your balance pie, you noticed that a huge piece is work, but you'd rather it was with family—or vice versa. Take some time to brainstorm how you can begin to make small changes that will increase the neglected piece. That could be something like having a sit-down breakfast before work and school a couple times a week (where everyone who's able takes turns or helps—I'm not suggesting adding more to your plate alone) or implementing designated no-electronics times (yes, for everyone including you) and do something together.

This isn't a process that you'll complete in five minutes, a day, or a month. It takes time to reconfigure and align your inner self with your actions and behaviors. This will be something that you start small and then build upon until it's second nature and no longer a conscious effort.

It's also not about perfection or the lofty idea that by being self-actualized, your life will somehow be devoid of bumps in the road or some good old-fashioned universe smackdown. But when you've polished off your internal gems, instead of being filled with a lackluster defense, you realize you already have a treasure trove of experience and self-worth to either mitigate damage or employ an efficient recovery plan.

When you're able to transition to self-actualization, it feels more like living authentically and embracing the things that make you unique, including—and especially—the quirky ones. This is the feeling I'm talking about when I say to embrace your inner boss bitch! This is the person who shines the light on their gems, whatever the color, and then comfortably stands up for what they believe in their hearts with a fist full of diamonds.

Other ways to help you determine if you're self-actualized includes the following:

- You're not afraid of the future or the unknown.

- You have the ability to live independently from the opinions of others as well as establish a comfortable relationship with solitude.

- The friendships in your life feel meaningful as well as appropriately reciprocated.

- You share an abundance of kindness and compassion with others—and yourself—and are able to practice acceptance.

- You don't get all wadded up over spontaneous situations.

- You take moments to experience "awe"; this can also be described as euphoria, joy, and wonder.

- You make time to be creative in whatever speaks to your heart—I don't care if you just glue glitter to paper, that counts.

Diamonds, Rubies, and Emeralds, Oh My!

When you discover your treasure trove of gems, it makes sense that they are all different shapes, sizes, colors, and types, but they all contribute to your overall person. Another way to think of this is like those giant pictures that all combine to make a recognizable face, but when you get really close, you can see that each "pixel" is actually a much smaller photo of the same face in different settings or moments.

All of these small photos in various states come together to create a singular self-image. The same is true of our chest of gems. All of the emeralds, rubies, diamonds, sapphires, topaz, black onyx, quartz crystal, and so on, can represent different aspects of your inner sparkle.

If it's helpful, you can actually list out some gem colors and then assign an associated feeling or idea to help represent all that is within you. For instance, your rage could easily be rubies, but rubies could also represent love and desire. Sometimes our emeralds might be grown from moments of jealousy, but they could also represent freshness and relaxation. Deep blue, like sapphire, can be depression but also confidence; light blue topaz could be rejuvenation.

The point is, the treasure chest is brimming with everything you need to feel like a rich bitch. There's probably even a gem encrusted crown in there with your name on it in diamonds which are clearly our definitive glimmer and glam.

So, even when we feel like we look like a hot mess laundry turd on the outside, we are sparkling like crazy on the inside. Self-actualization is not only letting your treasure shine through the seams, but also sharing that gorgeous light with the world authentically and unapologetically.

Things Don't Happen for a Reason

I believe that every single event in life happens in an opportunity to choose love over fear. –Oprah Winfrey

Oprah is obviously a genius sage, and her thoughts about challenges sum it up nicely. When we experience difficult situations and overwhelming heartbreak, it's incredibly hard to lift our heads up from all consuming darkness. I have a hard time with the idea of "choosing joy" over other emotions because that seems overly simplified and a way to encourage some of the negative coping mechanisms discussed earlier.

But choosing love over fear isn't a simple ask, and it means something deeper. When you choose love, first and foremost, it's a signal to your brain that you value yourself enough to begin to try to pick up the pieces. Choosing love over fear doesn't mean putting on a happy face when confronted with hardships; it means recognizing that dealing with the situation in a way that is healthy for your mind, body, and spirit.

Things don't just happen for a reason nor are hardships placed in your path because you have somehow attracted or caused them. I know it seems like the universe has a sniper rifle aimed at your chest sometimes, and we joke about the singular vision of her goal to destroy our lives, but in reality, it's just a way to try to put some blame on the random and extremely difficult things we go through.

Have you ever been going through something terrible, and someone says something like, "it will all work out for the best" or "everything happens for a reason," and you're instantly enraged? These blanket type responses or ways of thinking trivialize traumatic events that also have the power to change the landscape of your life. And in a way, it makes you feel responsible as if it was somehow your fault.

I'm not talking about direct consequences to specific decisions and actions that result in a positive or negative situation. When you've put hard work into something and achieve a goal, the reason is you. If you've made less-than-great decisions that culminated in a negative result, that is also for a reason. (Here, I don't mean violence or assault; I mean if you show up late to work every day and then lose your job, it's not for a random reason.)

In her book, *It's OK That You're Not OK*, Devine (2017) discusses the idea of grief and how as a culture we behave absolutely fucking bonkers over it. It makes us so uncomfortable that we say the weirdest shit to people going through horrific experiences. Her specific example is the tragedy of losing her husband in a freak accident and having a really challenging time with people telling her it was "for a reason," "it will work out for the best," or that she somehow "attracted" this sort of event.

The point here is that whatever the event or situation, the reason doesn't matter nearly as much as how you respond. You don't need to pretend to be excited or grateful to learn a lesson. I could have gone my entire life never learning some of the lessons graciously bestowed upon me.

However, everything that happens to us can be something to learn from. We don't need to be thankful for the opportunity, but if we want to continue to love ourselves and share our sparkling spirits with the world, we do need to figure out a way to live with it. One of those ways is to deconstruct and analyze what's going on and see if there is anything we can learn that we'll then have in our arsenal for the next time—cause there will be next time; there always fucking is.

As craptastic as it is, these are also some of the moments that if we live through them and come out the other side in some kind of person-shaped lump, they only add to the strength within. That strength may currently feel like it's buried, but girl, it's in there; I promise.

Just as a living, breathing woman, you have already lived through some sort of hell as that is the nature of things. That is the ugly truth. But your tragedy doesn't need to define you or keep you locked in some sort of cage. What does your inner self want? What is your boss bitch screaming at you from behind bars?

Chapter 7:

An Invisible Force

Speaking of feeling trapped, one thing that is certainly holding your glorious boss bitch hostage is fear. The idea of fear is a tricky monster because we behave in many ways to circumnavigate undesirable altercations or situations out of perception. We think that if we behave a certain way, that will prevent a disastrous or harmful result.

But what is that fear really saving you from? Seriously, take a minute to think about it. For example, you're afraid of being called a bitch at work, so you ignore the rude way in which a coworker—we'll call her Tina—composes requests via email. Since you don't respond in a way to provide corrective behavior feedback, you avoid having a potential confrontation.

However, every time you receive an email from Tina, you experience an automatic stress reaction because you already know it's going to piss you off, but you're not going to do a damn thing about it. These daily stressors add up and contribute to your inevitable tipping point.

That's just one simple example, but if you're doing this all over the place—at home, work, school, the grocery store—you're slowly packing away and stuffing down your identity out of fear.

Fear Factor

What even is fear? In general, it's supposed to be a survival mechanism that lets us know when things are shady as fuck, and we should run or fight. It's definitely not meant to keep you in some sort of walking, comatose potato state.

Fear is tricky to nail down because it can be both acute and chronic, obvious and subtle, and conscious and subconscious. Well, that's great—sort of reminds me of trying to get a piece of shell out of a cracked egg and right when your finger is over it and you press down, the slippery bastard slides away or squishes around. I'm sure my children have eaten many an eggshell after I whispered, "Fuck it," and proceeded with the next ingredient.

When fear is in the driver's seat, our minds and bodies are along for the ride:

- Physically, we've got all hands on deck: Our brain signals a nervous system response, which gets all excited, flooding our bodies with hormones (like we don't have enough of that roller coaster already going on), and causing things like blood pressure, heart rate, and breathing to increase. This is the classic flight or fight response.

- All of our muscles actually tighten up and energy stores are released (glucose) as well as white blood cells (an immune system response) and calcium.

- Our thought process becomes impaired and thinking things through logically becomes incredibly difficult. When you're living in fear of living authentically, this is prolonged zombification of your brain. It also becomes difficult to use fear for its design—survival—because it has become numb to constant exposure.

- Another response our body will have in face of fear is to freeze. Obviously, there are predator-prey scenarios that make sense to make as little movement as possible (like if *Jurassic Park* is to be believed and the T. rex can only sense movement). But think about the implications of this: With fear, you can be frozen in place. If you're not moving, not only are you not living your life in the present, enjoying what's around you, but you're also not growing or allowing opportunity for change and evolution.

How Fear Is Strangling You

Fear holds us back, mentally, emotionally, and physically, and having a prolonged fear response creates trained reactions to situations that we are frequently exposed to. This can make it even harder to deal with because our brain stops taking a pause between the stimulus and response, preventing evaluation over whether or not we actually want to keep responding in the same way.

How do you know if fear is holding you back if your brain has removed the review of the input-reaction pathway? I could be sitting here, talking about fear holding you back, and you're thinking: *I'm not afraid of shit*. And yet, your inner boss bitch and genuine self is actually trapped behind barriers of fears that have solidified and is now virtually silent.

There are some common distinguishable characters of being held back by fear:

- When you live from a place of fear, you don't spend any time analyzing decisions or thinking a problem through—especially a repeat offender. You have an automated response to potential stress inducing scenarios.

- If you constantly stay within your comfort zone, fear may be the reason. It will advocate against and prevent us from trying new things or venturing into unknown territory—literally and figuratively. "Comfort zone" doesn't necessarily equal "a place where you're happy and feel good." Remaining within a particular boundary could also mean being stuck in painful situations.

- When we come to a crossroad—not for the purpose of making supernatural deals—we theoretically have a handful of directions from which to choose. Fear is that adorable little British worm from *Labyrinth* saying, "No! Don't go that way! Never go that way!" (Henson, 1986, 20:53). The message is packaged as kind and helpful; complete with a warm cup of tea. However, with fear, we tend to only see the downside of choices and don't even consider what the positives outcomes may be.

- Connected with not being allowed to mentally weigh options and only seeing the downside, our intuition is also all jacked up. What is your gut trying to tell you? When fear is rumbling the loudest, it's incredibly difficult to hear what else your intuition is trying to tell you.

- When you're held back with fear, the perceived chance of failure or rejection overshadows the possibility of success. You don't strive for new goals or try to make any dreams come true. You don't meet new people which cuts off the opportunity to make new friends, build new relationships, or make new contacts that could also lead to new possibilities.

- Other signs that you're being held back by fear include: procrastination, a tendency to be a people pleaser, being an incredibly strict rule follower, actively rejecting others before they have a chance to reject you creating almost an outward seemingly fearless persona, but actually alone and fearful, plagued with self-doubt especially over what others will think about you, excuses abound when talking about goals, you are inflexible and would never be described as "go with the flow," and being deeply avoidant of the possibility of hardship.

- If we're open to taking a closer look at ourselves, we might also find that we're afraid of inadequacy, uncertainty, missing out (FOMO), losing control, and being judged.

Is This All in My Head?

There is a big difference between realistic and imagined or perceived fear, but it's not always easy for us to tell the difference, especially if our brains and bodies are on autopilot. Everything then gets lumped into the "realistic" category and treated in a similar manner.

We're also really great at making wide, sweeping, if-then type of thought cascades: If this terrible thing happens, then of course, so will this next thing, and followed up by the next negative thing, and on and on until we're shaking our heads, "Nope," and backing away from the opportunity.

Analyzing a situation in full is not a bad thing, but it's also important to allow for the possibility of success or positive changes. There should additionally be some stopgaps in there that allow you to stop at each "thing" and look at the possible outcomes, both positive and negative. Okay, so what *if* the first terrible thing happens? That doesn't necessarily mean we're on a runaway train to doomsville.

When we're talking about embracing our boss bitch, depending on what that means for you, there could be both realistic and imagined fears to deal with. If you show up for work and stop taking shit from everyone and someone calls you a bitch, so what? No, seriously, what is the fallout?

If you're approaching the situation in a way that is assertive and honest, you're not doing anything wrong. Whoever is reacting to you with a disproportionate response is the person who should feel shame, not you. So, why do we still fear that situation?

Of course I still get nervous when faced with conflict. Activity searching it out isn't what I'm suggesting. However, even though I'm nervous about the possible conflict, since I've approached the situation in a way that is in congruence with my inner self and supported by my boss bitch, I trust that I'll get through the brief moment of being uncomfortable, and the result will be better for me than the prolonged suffering that would result from not speaking up.

That's the other thing that fear robs us of: the ability to distinguish proportion. The amount of time you might fear a situation is so much longer than it takes for the entire scenario to play out.

Have you ever had a presentation to give, work or school, and basically since the first utterance of this inevitably, you're all twisted up? You spend weeks or months dreading the moment of your speech, procrastinating the task, experiencing upset stomach, diarrhea, and nightmares.

Then it's the day, you're sick, sweating, and stammering... and then... it's over in 15 minutes. Maybe it was excruciating, but it's over, no one even cares, and you think: *Okay, so I didn't pass out and die; thanks for all that fucking hype up, body. Maybe cool it down a bit for the next one.*

This Is Scary AF!

We've already done some practicing at self-examination and analysis so this builds on that skill you're developing. You may also have already stumbled upon some of your fears through the exercises in Chapter 5.

If you've spent any time dealing with anger issues or the tendency to explode when things go wrong, you're probably familiar with the idea that some of the emotions we experience are really just surface level reactions. Many of the things we get super pissed over are due to underlying fears.

When I've screamed profanities through the phone at insurance carriers, yeah, I was super fucking angry, but why exactly? Well, they were the reason why my family wouldn't get needed care or medication or it would have been an extreme financial hardship, especially for a single mom with two babies. Without the necessary healthcare, that could prolong or exacerbate the pain my child was experiencing. Well, that's basically the most terrifying thing in the world. So, yeah, insurance call center person, I'm fucking irate!

To start working on identifying your fears, you can think about the things that make you angry and frustrated. Make a short list of your top three to five things that make you the most angry and then using a technique similar to the association waterfall, you can make links down the chain:

1. The morning drop-off drives me fucking crazy.

2. No one knows how to drive or follow the rules.

3. I'm letting my precious babies out into this traffic.

4. What if someone accidently hurts them?

5. What if I accidentally run over a child or other person?

6. What if I accidentally—or on purpose—ram my vehicle into the back of the car in front of me?

7. I'm going to be late to work—again.

8. I cannot lose this job; financially, I couldn't swing it.

9. I hate showing up to work frazzled.

So, from the idea of being irritated at a basic morning routine, there are fears for the safety of your loved ones, the safety of others, and financial security. In the moment, it seems more like it's "Tina, who won't get out of the fucking way!" but in reality, it's much deeper.

Anger and frustration are usually easy to link with some sort of fear, but we also tend to practice avoidance, both for specific scenarios as well as decision-making out of fear. We also tend to make choices that err on the side of caution so as not to end up alone. Oftentimes, we categorize ourselves as introverted or extraverted, however the clinging to those labels may be out of fear—fear of rejection for the first, fear of being alone for the later.

More questions you can ask yourself to help sort out and identify fears are listed below (Borbala, 2020):

- Do you constantly think or worry about what other people think of you? What is your biggest fear related to this?

- Are you happy *and* thriving in your job? Would you leave if you could? If yes, what's holding you back?

- When comforted by someone in a position of authority, how do you feel? If it makes you uncomfortable, why do you think that is?

- Are you comfortable being alone? Do you actively carve out alone time or do you avoid it at all costs? If so, why do you think that is?

- Are you receptive to or against change? Why is change scary?

- Do you allow yourself to be vulnerable? Never? Only with people you trust? With whoever, whenever?

- What are your feelings about uncertainty—the unknown? Can you engage in thinking about possibilities or speculative futures without freaking out?

- The truth is out there—do you avoid it? Are there some things you'd rather just not know? If so, why do you avoid seeking or identifying the truth?

- Do you have any dreams or goals that continually call out to you and plague your days with constant berating that you actively ignore? What about these dreams are scary?

- Are you an expert level avoider? Does your schedule and routine make allowances to specifically avoid certain places, situations, or people? Is this to combat annoyance and frustrations or are there underlying fears associated with this behavior?

Another way to help identify fears is to conduct thought experiments—probably with some wine and a trusted friend for good measure and opportunities for dark humor—to play out "what's the worst that could happen" scenarios. For instance, if you're afraid to make the move to a new career, what's the worst that can happen? *Can* being the operable word.

If you have money saved, it's a seamless transition to a different employer, or you have a supportive partner who also earns an income, the *worst* that can happen is probably not financial ruin, destitution, or homelessness. The worst that could happen is probably more along the lines of being miserable in our daily work life, but what's the best that can happen? Does the best outweigh the realistic worst possible?

However, if you don't have that financial stability, it's more of a risk in some way, or you'll need to be in a couple months' worth of a transition, then the worst possible outcomes may include things like losing your home and that is a real and significant concern that deserves a ton of evaluation.

When you're analyzing your fears, it's important to examine them within the realm of what is actually possible and not defer to your incredibly active imagination. This also goes for when you're determining possible solutions.

Chapter 8:

Make Fear Your Bitch

I know that actually doing self-examination and trying to identify your fears is something that is scary all by itself. For a long time, these types of personal investigations and deep dives into my life left me feeling incredibly depressed, trapped, and overwhelmed—but only at first.

The pain that comes from these types of exercises would always start in the pit of my stomach, until moving up my throat, and making it difficult to speak or swallow. Tears would well up and brim over the edge, almost like a little metaphor all on their own. I've cried silent, sobbing, ugly, mascara-running-down-my-face tears.

I've also shed tears of joy and from laughing so hard (I miss you, Molly), I thought I might not be able to breathe—or pee my pants, especially after having my beautiful boys. I mean, I love them terribly, but I wasn't expecting to fear laughing—or sneezing, jumping, coughing, lifting—you get it.

But the aftermath of shedding tears is a familiar feeling of release. You feel empty, but in a good way; in a way that makes you ready to receive ideas and changes. This is the state you need to find to embrace the real and decide how you want to live your life.

It's okay to be afraid of the process—of what you might find or to give honest words to the feelings and situations you're dealing with. But you need to be brave when facing yourself: Nothing changes if nothing changes.

The state or feeling of fear is not a decision; you're not "choosing not to be afraid." You're actually doing something much braver: examining your fears and making a conscious choice to embrace who you are despite being afraid.

It's sort of like when you get on a roller-coaster. You know it will be terrifying, but the resulting feeling will be exuberance. As soon as the ride starts, does your fear vanish? As soon as the plummet starts, are you no longer afraid? Shit no. But you're strapped in, and there's no getting off this ride.

What if You Weren't Afraid?

A lot of people are afraid to say what they want. That's why they don't get what they want. –Madonna

Think about it. What if you weren't afraid? I'm not talking about ignoring, moving past, or conquering it. I mean, pretend the fear doesn't exist at all; pretend there are no consequences to any decisions.

What's the first thing you would do? Jump out of an airplane? Punch someone in the face? Rob a bank? Perform at a rock concert? Go back to school? Write a book? Tell someone you loved them? Tell someone you don't love them anymore? Swim with sharks? Live on a deserted island? Take a year off of everything and backpack around the world? Build houses in another country? Quit your job? Run an ultra marathon? Have a baby? Ask for some help? Spend a day without filtering your thoughts before they flew out of your mouth? Live off the grid? Buy a ticket for the next billionaire jaunt into space? Go to a beginner's pointe class for adults? Pack your shit up and move out? Get a divorce? Call an old friend? Stalk a celebrity?

What would you do?

Go big here! Get creative with it—I'm sure you notice some of the above examples are a little out there but don't hold back. Exercising our creativity is underrated and not promoted nearly enough. We're constantly bombarded with messages about exercising our bodies, but our minds need it, too.

So this is a great exercise for a handful of reasons; one of them being a self-examination of possible fear-based thinking patterns, but the other is giving over our brains to creative and ridiculous thoughts. It needs it!

Feel free to write these things down in your journal and add to the list as things pop up. Sometimes, especially if we're a little rusty in the imagination and creativity department, it's hard to jump start the engine. But once it's going, it will run on its own in the background and filter inputs under a new scope. Maybe you notice someone else doing something interesting, read about an adventure, or see a show or movie that inspires you.

After you've made a list of the above, focus your lens onto your existing life, and complete the following exercise:

- Think about one typical day, start to finish, including all the activities and people you interact with.

- You could either think about a specific day—perhaps a particular day you know had those moments of fear-based choices—or just a generalized day. Close your eyes if you have to; that actually helps me visualize the moment better or access memories.

- Break the day up into smaller sections that will be easier to analyze; this can be by hours (6:30 a.m. to 8:00 a.m., 8:00 a.m. to 12:00 p.m., etc.), events (before work, work hours, after work, early evening, evening), or some other schedule that reflects your life. Maybe you don't work or have a flexible, inconsistent schedule; maybe you don't have children; maybe you have pets to consider. The point is, this works for whatever your schedule or life looks like. Just break it up into sections that work for you.

- For each section of your day, think about the choices you make. Don't skip over things that seem like an automatic action or just part of the routine. That's exactly what we're trying to challenge. Do you put almond milk in your coffee instead of creamer? Do you even like almond milk? Are you actually allergic to regular milk or is it a choice to cut calories? Do you need to cut 70 calories out of your morning coffee or is there any fear about food choices and body image that plague your day start to finish without even realizing it?

- Try thinking like a four-year-old and ask yourself "why" about everything and don't stop until it feels weird, or you've settled on an answer.

- For all your answers as to why you make the choices you do, sort out the ones that need a little further investigation or are clearly made out of fear. If it was me, I'd use a fun color-coded system.

- When you have those specific moments and choices throughout the day, take each one and write what you want to or would do instead if there was nothing else to consider—no hurt feelings, no dire consequences, no pounds gained, no money lost, no pride.

- Picture this same day again, but when you go through the day in your mind, replace the usual choices with your list of alternate reactions and choices.

- After you've "lived" through this alternate reality day, are there any moments that stand out as being instant relief? Does changing anything provide alleviation, even momentarily?

If your initial thought when completing this exercise is that you would get in your car, drive away, and never look back, I get it. I hear that in my heart. I've been in the car with the engine idling ready to flee the scene. But take a little U-turn, come back to the questions, and try to see if you can come up with something.

If you really can't, that's important to realize, and I would also strongly encourage reaching out for help; either from a doctor, friend, or other supportive service. I don't want to pretend that we can fix everything on our own or that some of us aren't in situations so dark, we're not even sure where to turn our faces to get a glimpse of light. If that's truly where you are, please don't hesitate to acknowledge it.

What if You Were Still Afraid but Did It Anyway?

I don't care what you think about me. I don't think about you at all. –Coco Chanel

That's sort of where we're trying to get—Chanel I-could-give-a-fuck level. Two of the biggest fear cheerleaders in our way are caring about what other people think and not being good enough. I mean, come on, that's only two things! What's the BFD? Alright, yes, these are two crazy, huge, boulders in the path that basically encompass every faucet of our daily lives and being. So, yeah, they're monumentally in our way.

The feeling of fear isn't really a choice; you're not going to make the fears you've spent a lifetime developing, nurturing, and giving free reign to go away. If you've been waiting to not "be afraid" before doing something or making a decision, girl, that's not happening.

It's sort of the same as motivation. If we spend a bunch of time waiting to "be motivated," nothing actually gets done because you can't conjure that shit out of nowhere. Meanwhile, time keeps going, deadlines approach, goals die, and dreams fade.

We're building ourselves an enemies-to-lovers trope within the story of our lives. Fear is your enemy, for sure, but it's also secretly trying to tell you things. It just never got the memo to be cool about it; it's still stuck in third grade, putting gum in the hair of the girl it likes. Some of the things we fear the most are connected to some of our deepest dreams and desires.

With a family to support, a house to manage, and a career to foster, my plate was full. But since I had to drop out of school at an early age to have my children, I've always had a deep longing to continue my education. Fitting that in was never easy and there was plenty to be afraid of along the way: What if I lose my job? What if I'm not there when my kids need me? What if I ruin my finances with this investment? What if I don't have anything in common with the other students? What if I'm not smart enough to pass the class? What if I do this and waste a bunch of time? What if, what if, what if?

Well, now I'm almost finished with my doctorate degree. I didn't need one—I fucking *wanted* one. And I brought my fear along for the ride, sitting bitch, and trying to detour me. Fear's like that; it's selfish and wants you to spend all of your time thinking about it. That's why it's such a great control tactic. No matter who's wielding it, we already know fear, we're familiar with its voice, and we're conditioned to behave accordingly.

Fear may have shackled itself to your mind, but your body belongs to you, and fear will have to go wherever you make it.

So, what if you were afraid and did it—whatever *it* is—anyway?

Embrace the Real

I'm not trying to be overly simplistic; you may very well have a dickhead boss and being afraid to lose your job and financial stability is a very real possibility. That's valid and deserves recognition when deciding how you want to challenge fear-based thinking. But we want to start making some shifts in areas of your life where you can to ensure that not every part of your life is subjugated by fear.

There are a handful of techniques that will help you with fear-based thinking and embrace the real:

- Through the exercises in the last chapter and above, you've identified, recognized, and acknowledged fears.

- Although difficult, it's good practice to try to separate the feeling of fear from embarrassment; don't add power to fear by throwing a layer of shame over the top.

- Continuing to practice the "what's the worst that can happen" exercise is a great way to think about decisions, no matter how big or small.

- When you identify your fears and start critically reviewing them, you're preparing yourself for battle. It's the same as training for any other specialized skill. You don't jump into the ring and ask your opponent how to throw a punch; you spend considerable time training before going into a fight.

- Fear preys on our ability to mentally time travel. It aids us in seeing multiple futures that it colors with shades of darkness. Trying to stay in the present with your thoughts is helpful.

- No one is asking you to get off the couch and start running. That's why there are "couch to 5K" programs and intermediate levels all in between and beyond. Take small steps. These will add up; sometimes it's hard to see progress as it's happening, but it *is* happening.

- These are hard things you're working on. Recognizing fear and trying to step outside of normal, ingrained patterns is difficult so don't forget to celebrate victories.

- When you decide to take risks, don't jump in without thinking about it; bust out your journal and make a good old-fashioned pros and cons list. List realistic risks of your possible choices—good and bad.

- You're not perfect. Stop trying to be. I'm not even sure what that could possibly even mean—*perfect*. Your self-worth is not tied to failure or whether or not you're "enough." You just are; you are whole.

- Although it's hard, try to leave failure in the dust. Stop trying to dig that shit up.

- All that I'm asking you to do is a lot, I get it. So make sure to take some down time every so often. Just like your body needs a break, so does your brain.

Chapter 9:

Peas in a Pod

We are not singular beings, existing within a vacuum. Our relationships and various environments—work, home, social—factor into self-discovery and dealing with fears. It's important to realize that we can do all the work in the world within ourselves, but if we don't consider the outside influence of the people around us, especially our loved ones, we're only partially doing the work.

These relationships are very important; they make life worth living. But some of our automatic behavior responses and subsequent feeling like shit on the inside are due to habitual relationship dynamics.

This isn't always someone's direct intent. The people who love us would probably feel incredibly bad if they knew how much some continued patterns negatively affect us deep in our souls—but that's also part of the problem because it prevents us from speaking up. We don't want to make people feel bad, hurt feelings, or feel like we blew something out of proportion.

I think some of our biggest fears actually stem from a place of love. We fear hurting others because we love them, but in avoiding certain topics or actions, it's causing internal damage that will ultimately affect our friends and family negatively as well.

One Is the Loneliest Number

Is it? Is one the loneliest number? Some days—or maybe just minutes or hours—it seems like the luckiest number. Women are incredibly self-sufficient, can basically do everything, and would like one, quiet, God damned minute to themselves for peace and quiet. The idea of one being lonely was probably an idea created by someone who needed (wanted) another person to take care of them.

Why is it our job to not only take care of ourselves, but also a handful of other people while running a household, working, and showing up all smiles to every other facet of our lives?

Imagine it: You and you alone—what a wonderful, blissful world it would be. The noise would recede, pressures would release, muscles would relax. Of course, we love our people and being a singular soul floating around in the world would probably not ultimately make us happy. How do we find some kind of balance between tranquility and noise?

I have a couple secret, solitary locations that only I can access at any time. These are places within my mind that I have built, one through a guided meditation exercise with a spirit guide medium, and the other was just the first place that popped in my head when someone said, "Go to some place relaxing in your mind."

These types of mental happy places can be beneficial to retreat to for a variety of situations:

- coming home from a long day and needing a few minutes to transition from work to homelife

- having a medical procedure of some sort (MRI, dental work, biopsy, anything you're semi-awake for, or just waiting around somewhere that makes you nervous or uncomfortable)

- daily meditation practices (if you're into that sort of thing)

- nightly unwind bedtime routine

- anytime you need to clear your mind

- whenever you're feeling stressed, anxious, or nervous

- you need a couple of alone minutes—even if you can't physically be alone

For me, these are spots where I can really only fully occupy if I close my eyes so I'm not recommending for something like being stuck in traffic or meetings with your zoom camera on. You'll need a different technique for something like that.

My quick go-to mental spot is a secluded beach. There's a 300-foot section of sand that backs up against a tall cliff, accessible only by boat or a skinny staircase that winds down from a cliff house you can't see from the beach. The cove is closed in around all sides except what faces out to the ocean. Facing the ocean and to the left is an outcropping of rocks that form structures in the water (sort of like The Arch in Cabo San Lucas, Mexico). In my version, there is also a little cave that exists within the rock formation with a tall ceiling and is almost perfectly round (like being inside a snow globe).

When I close my eyes and access this spot, sometimes I'm sitting in a lounge chair or on a blanket, under a large beach umbrella or giant floppy hat, and concentrate on pushing my feet through the warm sand, brushing my heels against the slightly wet sand that's always just a few inches deep. I know what hot sand feels like as a real memory so I can easily transfer that sensation to this imaginary landscape. Sometimes, I explore the cave and imagine what the water sounds like from inside the rocks. Other times, I'll wade out into the water. I can picture this scene with a full, bright sun, wandering clouds, or easy rain storm. I can add a cold drink, sweating in a glass, probably a pina colada. The only sounds are the water, maybe a little wind, and birds.

If imagination is difficult for you or you have a hard time picturing things in your mind, you're welcome to my place. I won't even know you're there.

Your Mental Oasis

- What's the first place that comes to mind when you think of someplace relaxing and tranquil? This can be outside or inside, but try to shy away from an actual place that you inhabit—real places have real problems (and mess), and we're trying to get away from that for a minute.

- Build some walls of some kind around you. In my example, I use the landscape to close in a space, but it's still open to the ocean and sky. The idea here is to make it secure but also enough room to breathe. You could use a forest, mountains, stacks within a library, actual walls, and so on. Even if your spot is a wide-open meadow or ranchland, put some mountains or something out in the distance and create a circle around your location.

- Pick one sensation at a time to bring into your oasis. I always start with the hot sand. That is an instantaneous connection for me that brings me straight to the cove. So, for me touch is the most direct route, but you could also use familiar smells or sounds. Choose something that's easy for you!

- Add other sensations to your vision as you get comfortable. What does everything sound like? What does it feel like? Is there grass? Is it wet? Are there insects or other nature sounds? Are there sounds of pages turning or candles with wooden wicks crackling? As you practice getting to your location, experiment with adding in other things. I didn't always have the little cave to explore, but at some point added it.

- Do you have a spot? Now go there—regularly. This takes practice and repetition to create a space that eternally exists and is always waiting in perfect, pristine condition.

The Power of One

There exists within a driving force that only you can access. If it helps to visualize that power as a shining orb or like a star within your hands, do so. Put it in a mental oasis—the same one for relaxation or different one, whichever works for you. That way you know exactly where to find it and grab ahold of it whenever you need.

That driving force is what fuels our passions; it's what stimulates and encourages growth. We're bombarded with negativity throughout the entire day, but if you try to focus that energy into your driving force, it doesn't need to distinguish between positive and negative; it needs only to be power without connotation.

So whether your power is being charged up via positive or negative feelings and situations, the resulting driving force gives us an extra urge that we can decide to channel for success.

Family Knots

Our families are a gift, bless their hearts, but they can really fuck up our lives. I want to say that is generally not intentional nor malicious. It's just the byproduct of sharing our lives with other people who have their own set of needs and desires.

Unfortunately for women in general (or one of the partners in a relationship or singularly), we tend to take on the brunt of the work and responsibility when it comes to caring for everyone and everything. We basically have seven full-time jobs where everything is equally demanding and important.

We are expected to work tirelessly and oftentimes thanklessly for our loved ones. There is somehow a lofty idea of selflessness that sets us up for failure. We can't keep all the balls in the air, spinning perfectly, while also taking care of our own mental, emotional, and physical needs.

For some reason, there is also a double standard for family: We let them get away with treating us like we wouldn't let anyone else get away with. This concept is really difficult for most, but why does it make it okay because someone is family? Personally, I think it makes it worse.

Whether you have children, a partner, parents, siblings, other relatives, or not, family dynamics can be very challenging to deal with and the path of least resistance often prevails regardless of the consequences to you personally. Even the dead can still reach beyond the grave into our lives and dictate our actions. How crazy is that?

There is a difference between being there as a supportive figure and being run over. I'm not talking about when you have an imbalance of need and abilities. For instance, taking care of people with disabilities, aging family, other medical reasons, or young babies and children that can't do anything for themselves.

When does taking care of someone else cross the line into being taken advantage of? I think this answer is one you already know deep in your heart. When you feel like you don't know who you are anymore and have utterly lost yourself, it's time to critically assess through self-examination but also by looking closely at relationships and what you do for others.

In your journal, you might take a page—or 40—to list specific loved ones and what you do for them on a regular basis. These aren't all bad things; it enriches our lives to help people we love, but everything is better in balance. It's helpful to write it down and then look at that long and seemingly never-ending list. It's really no wonder why you feel depleted and at your wit's end; look at everything you're doing for everyone but yourself.

The practice of self-examination and embracing your inner boss bitch doesn't need to be restricted to you alone. It's perfectly reasonable and absolutely awesome to be you *and* encourage your family to embrace themselves as individuals. By the nature of things, that might mean you have some internal household clashes, but it's worth taking the time to sort through those situations and find compromises that work for everyone.

For those of us that are lucky to have a supportive family, it is also okay to reciprocate; just know where your own boundaries are and embrace them.

#Relationshipgoals

Many of us seek companionship to share our lives with whatever that means to you from a partnership perspective. But because of practices like showing our lives on social media and trends like #relationshipgoals, we often find ourselves stuck in comparison mode, leaving us feeling like something is lacking.

It can appear that for some reason unbeknownst to us, what we have with our significant other is somehow lacking when we try to measure up our reality with what "reality" is presented via social channels.

The idea that social media portrayal versus reality doesn't always match up isn't new information. But it's worth mentioning as a reminder. When we experience feelings of lack, our thoughts can downward spiral, and we leave out those little details when we can see how "perfect" everyone else's life looks.

All we see are the end photos; what we don't see are the stories behind them. Maybe you come across a photo of a friend and their partner sharing a loving embrace, looking like they're dancing in the kitchen while making dinner, and enjoying an intimate smile. It's tagged #reltionshipgoals and looks like they can conjure the magic of a moment as mundane as making dinner.

Your first reaction might be to go, "Ahhh, that's so sweet. I wish we had that." But think about it a little more: Who the fuck is taking that picture? Did these two put the timer on and then pose for this? Were they doing a video and happened to capture this "authentic" and "genuine" moment? It's more weird, right? And to go further, you happen to know that your friend is going through a really hard time with their partner so it feels even more off. Sometimes we just need to take a pause to think to stop the comparison avalanche.

As with our family, our partners greatly influence our behaviors. One common way is that we can tend to hide behind them. A relationship should be balanced; sure, there might be ups and downs where you take turns being the driving force or supportive role, but it should balance back out.

Our partners can dominate your sense of self in a variety of ways:

- They may be the reason you do or don't work or have a specific career.

- Some partners dictate who you spend free time with.

- A partner "sharing" in raising children or a household may continually challenge the way you do things.

- Partners can sometimes be incredibly needy with attention and don't practice their own self-sufficiency or cultivate friendships outside of your relationship.

- Your partner might not be receptive to speaking openly and honestly, creating a dynamic in which it is difficult to be vulnerable and share things about yourself.

- Partners can manipulate you into feeling like the bad guy or guilt trip you into doing what they want over anything you want or need.

- Some partners may feel their only job in the relationship or household is to provide financially.

- When our partners are also struggling, either with work or other personal problems, it's common for us to shrink down and make sure not to cause extra stress or issues for them.

- Just like us with ours, partners can have challenging relationship dynamics within their family that spill over into yours.

Whether you find yourself the main motivator or unspoken member, you can still be losing yourself with either too much on your plate in the former or silently fading away in the latter. In either situation, are you really living? Don't you want to be with someone who inspires you to be, do, and grow more?

When we're ready to embrace our inner boss bitch, it can seem like a complete 180 to our loved ones. We don't really want anyone to think of us as a "total bitch," but that's especially true with our partners. That's why having some open communication about the process you're attempting is a good idea. Letting them know upfront that you feel like you need to make some changes or do some deep diving can help you feel supported in the process as well as make it not seem like such a shocking change.

During self-evaluation, when you continually find that your troubling answers circle around your partner, this can be very challenging. You may be in a situation that feels impossible to change or leave. I'm also not asking you to do anything that would put yourself in danger.

Safety is the first priority; if you need help, please reach out to someone.

Posse

Our friendships also have an external force on how we act and whether we stuff things down or make compromises and allowances for various behaviors. I'm sure you've had all kinds of friendships over your life; I certainly have. I've had friends that were (and are) some of the best; who have my complete trust and I can be my most authentic self without a filter (looking at you, Amanda).

I've also had friends that hurt my feelings continuously or clearly didn't respect my time or compassion. These ones can be tricky because a lot of the time, they are friends you've had for a long time and feel like a permanent fixture in your life. Much like your family, it feels like you're stuck with them so might as well just let them dictate the terms. Actually taking the step to cut these people loose can be heartbreaking and incredibly difficult.

Our friendships should be given just as much time in the evaluation category to make sure they really are something we should be nurturing. Friends are supposed to be the ones you turn to when your family and partner are driving you out of your fucking mind, and you just need a break. They're also honest and genuine with you and provide loving and supportive feedback.

That doesn't mean that the truth doesn't hurt. If you've been in a relationship that is toxic, you may have at least one friend who has been trying to tell you. At the same time, when you get out of that relationship, they won't be there with an "I told you so," but a bottle of wine and lots of bad ideas to get you through it.

Part of the definition of posse is "a group of people temporarily organized." This immediately conjures up memories of "brunch gone wrong" moments or other events where my group of friends was organized in the beginning, but things disintegrated into a shitshow after a few drinks. Temporarily organized indeed.

What this also can mean is that like jeans, there are some friendships we grow out of. That's perfectly okay. If they're relationships that are healthy with both people wanting to make it work, you'll find your way. But there are other friendships that have overstayed their welcome and no longer serve you in a balanced and supportive way.

It doesn't need to mean you no longer speak to someone or are angry with them. It doesn't mean you don't wish them well in life and hope that whatever happens for them makes them truly happy. But if you haven't realized it, our time and energy are already finite resources and continuing to allocate precious reserves on friendships that don't balance is an unnecessary drain.

Out of Office

Work relationships also factor into self-discovery as we spend a ton of time with these people either in person or virtually. When you were going through the self-evaluation section, work issues including specific events and people may have been a recurring source of angst.

Self-reflection and examination might lead you to reconsider your career or recognize that some of the anxiety you experience stems directly from your job.

It seems like our feelings around our jobs are the ones that can make us feel trapped quicker than the same types of feelings from family, friends, and partners because on some level we've accepted those relationships as nonnegotiable where jobs feel more like a choice.

Don't get caught in a panic spiral over being trapped in a job. For some, this is a natural thing to change and not overly challenging; you simply realize you're not happy and move on to another option. I think for many people though, not only is work a source of stress, sadness, and anxiety, but it's also not something you cannot easily change. It's important to realize where you fall on that spectrum.

That doesn't mean you can't make changes to make your daily life more emotionally and mentally manageable. This circles back to the way we deal with fears. There are small changes you may be able to make to help address recurring situations or you may decide that trying to change things at work would be more trouble than they're worth. I get it.

The important part in the beginning of a journey like the one you're on is to start small. You also have a home and social life that probably needs some attention that you can focus on making adjustments to with your inner boss bitch supporting your driving force.

Consequently, as you make changes in one area of your life, some of the other sections will also feel different. If you feel more like your authentic self at home or with friends, that alleviates some of the anxiety and stress you feel overall.

Chapter 10:

Back Off, Bitch!

You have to be able to set boundaries, otherwise the rest of the world is telling you who you are and what you should be doing. You can still be a nice person and set boundaries. –Oprah Winfrey

Did you really think we'd get through the whole book without talking about boundaries? These are so important! But also something people struggle with. They are probably also why one would be called a bitch more often than not.

Funny how people react when they're no longer able to steamroll over the top of you or always get what *they* want. If that's what it means to be a bitch, I'm fine with it.

If you're not going to listen to me, listen to Oprah.

Exsqueeze Me? Baking Powder?

Girl, you need some boundary power! You could be sitting there thinking, *What the fuck is she talking about?*

Boundaries are nothing more than invisible lines you've placed that let you—and others—know what is acceptable behavior. That's it. But they are important for mental and emotional health, developing autonomy, and letting your actual identity shine through.

We can have as many different boundaries as we need or want. They'll look and feel a little different in the various areas of your life and can change from person to person. You can have some basic one-size-fits-all boundaries as a base layer and build from there as needed.

These are fully within your control so you decide when to create, readjust, or remove them. They are not set in stone and can be renegotiated as needed. The important part, however, is that you have some. And that you enforce them.

When we don't have boundaries, this allows others to take advantage of us. Even if that's only a little in every part of our lives, that shit adds up, making you feel like you don't get to be who you are or is causing you sadness that you feel deeply but are unsure why.

Some signs you may be lacking in the boundary department include the following:

- You constantly feel like you've overcommitted your time, rarely having any time for yourself.

- Your inner dialogue is very critical.

- You would rate your self-esteem on the low side.

- It's really hard for you to say "no."

- When you help people with their problems, you tend to take ownership of them as well.

- You have multiple personalities that you use depending on the person you're with or situation you're in.

- As soon as I said "boundaries," your stomach filled with guilt butterflies.

- You constantly feel exhausted, overwhelmed, and burned out.

Easier Said Than Done

I'm not trying to say that creating boundaries is simple; they are incredibly difficult to define and consistently enforce. Some people are also very good at sneaking around our boundaries, coming in for a sneak attack.

Creating exceptions is also a slippery slope. If you've never applied these before and are trying to add some to your life, it will be confusing to people if you sometimes enforce them and let them slide at other times.

Changing the dynamic of any relationship is tricky and not without challenges. Family, friends, and coworkers are going about their daily lives per usual; it's you that's deciding to make some changes. This can cause things to go less smoothly at work and home. It's a little bumpy getting going, but eventually it will level out one way or another.

With loved ones—friends and family—it's worth taking the time to talk about it and let them know what you need upfront instead of randomly popping up with "no" all over the place. You're not a two-year-old; you're not saying it just to say it. There's a reason, it's important, and worth sharing.

This is another thing that can take some time and something that you can build on, starting small and making minor tweaks as you go.

The people who push back against your boundaries, challenge your attempt to create a healthier balance in a relationship, or respond with friction and confrontation deserve some attention from a critical review. Why are they so resistant? What did your boundary change for them?

What does this type of behavior in response say about those people? They are probably the ones benefiting the most from your willingness to forego personal needs and wants to help others. They are the ones counting on the idea that most people avoid confrontation and will acquiesce to many demands outside of what their responsibilities actually are to prevent uncomfortable conversations.

The people who have a problem with you making healthy choices for yourself are usually the ones trying to get away with something. I think children test this naturally; it's just part of growing up and that's not really what I mean. However, even young children start to get a hang of what they can do to get what they want including throwing a scene at the grocery store to embarrass Mom.

When you're setting and enforcing boundaries, you need to be ready to accept and deal with some uncomfortable situations and conversations. This is unavoidable but necessary to embrace your inner boss bitch and live authentically.

How to Build a Minefield

So how the heck are you supposed to do this anyway? Well, one way to tackle setting boundaries is sort of like setting goals: outline the small steps, be clear and concise on your desired outcome and what each step entails, practice, and grace (with yourself and others).

A step-by-step guide might look like this:

1. Determine where you want boundaries: define the problem and sketch out what's contributing to the situation.

2. Communicate directly without fluff to avoid ambiguity or wavering; your lines are clear to you but invisible to others unless you draw attention.

3. Don't let things slide; enforce what you've set up.

When we start talking about boundaries, does one specific friend come to mind? Do you already know someone you would consider has great boundaries? Why do you think that? What is it about them that gives off that impression? Do you have a negative view of them, or do you envy their ability to say no, prioritize time, and display confidence?

In general, I would say that most people, women especially, who have awesome boundaries are happy to share tips and tricks with others. This is also great if your circles cross (work, home, social) because they might already either have similar situations or insider knowledge of your life and where some boundaries would help.

So, what's stopping you from getting some ideas from a boundary role model? "Nothing" is the correct answer.

Be Assertive

There is a difference between assertiveness and aggressiveness. Boundaries and being assertive go hand in hand. Focusing on this distinction is helpful for people who are nervous about being overly aggressive or hurting feelings so that you are confident in your choices and aren't swayed by someone's reaction.

However, we can't control how people will react or feel. It's therefore important that you have embraced your boundaries in your heart, knowing that what you're asking for or rejecting is what *you* need.

Being assertive is about you, so using "I" statements is really helpful. Your tone, volume, and inflection also help with sounding conversational rather than confrontational. If you keep it conversational—no matter how aggressive or reactive the other person gets or how much you'd like to just start ripping someone a new one—this only solidifies your position, and the other person seems unhinged or unreasonable.

Try starting sentences with "I need" and "I feel." It's also helpful to stick to fact-based statements, especially at work. "I have completed the department's shared report every week on my own. This is supposed to be a collective task. I need help with preparing this moving forward." Take a minute to read that out loud and get an idea what I mean when I say tone, volume, and inflection matter. If you have teenagers, you already get it.

But some of the words in the above example lend themselves to infusing feelings into the statement and can put people on the defensive. "I have completed the department's shared report. This is a collective task. I need help preparing this moving forward." So, word choice is also something to keep in mind.

"No" Is Not a Bad Word

This is how I look at it: If it's a question, I can answer however I'd like, including—and *especially*—no. Some people have no problem asking for things; many count on the fact that it's uncomfortable to say no. When you want to say no, but you get a little bubble of guilt in your stomach, take a beat.

Why are you feeling guilty? Why don't you want to do the thing? This is where the self-examination really comes to the rescue because if you already know why (for example, it's better for your mental and emotional health), it makes it easier to ignore our stupid stomachs and say no.

You don't have to be rude about it; you can say "no, thank you" or you can offer an alternative, either something you can do or point them in the right direction. Having boundaries isn't about shutting down being helpful or kind; it's about making sure you're able to have the time and energy to invest in areas of your life that are meaningful.

If you're constantly saying yes to everything and everybody, you're essentially shrinking other pieces of your pie and devaluing your own needs and wants.

Saying no also doesn't need an accompanying speech as to why. Not everything requires an explanation nor does babbling away reinforce your assertiveness. Try to refrain from conjoining no with supportive evidence: "No, it's just that…" or "No, I would if I could but I (insert fake excuse here)."

As much as it's ready to roll right off your tongue, try to avoid adding "I'm sorry" to the end of your statement as well; unless the situation calls for it, and you're truly sorry. But apologizing for saying no is not doing you any favors.

All the Options

I had a manager who regularly talked down to the women in the department. But not me. One of the things I noticed was he had a tendency to come into the cubical space to give feedback or make requests. When he'd come to my area, instead of remaining sitting and looking up toward him, I would get up and face him to have the conversation. I would then slowly move forward, and his natural response was to back away out of my space. There were no challenging words, just clarification on what was being asked of me as I reaffirmed with posture that respectful conversation was appreciated.

What I'm saying here is body language is also a tool to help communicate to others: eye contact, body placement, posture, and refrain from fidgeting.

Other things to keep in mind include the following:

- Just like using "I" statements, try to avoid saying "You" statements.

- Unless you're using your phone as a list or otherwise supportive element to your conversation, put it down.

- It's important to keep it simple, but when we're talking about friends and family, it's better to explain some reasoning rather than avoiding the person all together.

Made by You, for You

The most important part of boundaries is that they are personally designed to fit your specific needs. My boundaries won't look like yours. These are meant to help you embrace your authentic self, helping you achieve your desired life dynamics. Your inner boss bitch is the perfect voice of reason and support in this effort.

They are not meant to hinder relationships, but they should help restructure any relationships where you feel less-than, overwhelmed, or underappreciated in any way. Boundaries are a tool to ensure the preservation of self and to allow for the space for you to breathe.

When you're working with adding, restructuring, or enforcing boundaries, these should be created within your own comfort zone and reflect what you currently need. They are flexible in that you can adjust them to what works the best for you in different stages of your life, career, and relationships.

But keep in mind, hanging out in our comfort zones is sometimes part of the problem and a little push past might be in order. If you think you have boundaries set up that are working and within your zone of comfort, but you still feel deep longing, overwhelm, hurt, frustration, lost, etcetera, take another critical look at your boundaries and whether a push—just a little one—is needed.

Chapter 11:

Haters Gonna Hate

I mean, right? Whenever you go down a self-improvement route, there will be haters heckling your empowerment. It usually boils down to them losing out in some way that was actually costing you time and energy as well as hampering your emotional and mental health. In my opinion, these people can fuck off. Good riddance.

Sometimes though, these are also people we're stuck with—including ourselves!

Pressure Points

Yes, other people will push back on boundaries, but the person to be wary of is yourself. We can make exceptions and naturally shy away from things that are uncomfortable. Girl, if you haven't figured it out, this whole business is going to be uncomfortable. But isn't the point that you're struggling in other areas and desperately need a change? You're already way past this stage, so technically, moving to uncomfortable is an improvement.

Get out of your own way for God's sake! A huge pressure point comes directly from the source of change so don't make allowances for anyone, especially yourself. We don't always do what's best for us or follow through with personal goals. That's also why starting with small changes is key to lasting effects. When we're uncluttering our lives, you don't jump straight into reorganizing cabinets and drawers; you first decide what's trash and get rid of it.

Also, your existing patterns and habits will naturally push back on boundaries you're trying to enforce—that's what *force* of habit means. If you're in the habit of saying yes to everything and helping everyone all the time, these things are part of your daily routine! Stop automatically going through the motions and resist the "go-with-the-flow" mentality.

Runaway Guilt-Trip Train

This train is a bitch, in a bad way. It pops out of nowhere and inhabits space it has zero right to. This is a hard one. I still have to actively tell myself over and over "this is not something you need to feel guilty about" for some situations.

The best way to combat this feeling is to have your foundation solid for all your "whys." Check yourself against feeling guilty. This emotion gives us lots of clues to our behavior, but it's not always a signal that you shouldn't be doing something.

When we feel like we're somehow disappointing others, the pit in our stomach swells to an enormous size. This connects to that common fear of not being enough. Honestly, this feeling almost gives me some faith in humanity because one our biggest sources of worry, guilt, and fear is not being enough to help others. In a way, that's sort of beautiful.

Even though it's natural to want to help and support your loved ones, if doing so is exacting a cost to your emotional and mental health, you need to find a balance.

To not let guilt get the best of you, try the following:

- Talk through it as if you were speaking to your best friend—bonus points for literally doing this.

- Ignore the guilty feeling, enforce your boundary or change, and see what happens—did the world end? Probably not. Take some time to realistically review perceived versus actual consequences.

- Forgive yourself—not for making informed, empowered, boss bitch decisions; forgive yourself for alloying these harmful patterns for so long that challenging them causes a guilty feeling.

Bon Voyage, Bitch

As much as we sometimes want to kick a relationship or situation to the curb, it's not always realistic. Most of the time, our jobs and coworkers are nonnegotiable.

And of course, we love our children, but my goodness, some days their true little-shit side comes out when they're being mischievous, sneaky, tricky, and funny—not funny "haha," funny like they're pulling one over on their parents—amiright? Gotta love 'em.

I'm sure you have relationships that are not only the root cause of some of your problems, but are at the same time not easily dissolved nor is that the desired result. Communication with our loved ones is important; they might not even realize they're causing blurred lines, pushing back on boundaries, and buying you one-way guilt-trip tickets.

However, others are very aware of their behaviors and intent—those who are deceitful and jealous—and they deserve a bon voyage outta your life if at all possible.

Triage

Can't live with 'em, can't kill 'em—so now what?

For the people that are a source of your stress and anxiety but who you also still want to be major fixtures in your life, communication and vulnerability are going to be your biggest allies. Usually, these are also people who love and respect us as well; they don't really want to be a source of negative energy.

Being open and honest with our "keep pile" of people is also a great way to help and encourage loved ones to embrace their inner boss bitch, too. Maybe they have no idea how to go about getting the things they need and want and have been using blunt force because they know no other way.

There is also power in time and space. Not everything needs an immediate response or course correction. If you have someone who is problematic but who you are also forced to work with, taking a breather, removing yourself from the situation, and examining your choices are helpful. Can a problem really not wait 5–10 minutes for you to review?

Breaking up the momentum of a situation can diffuse feeling forced into making decisions that are counterproductive to your authenticity. "Let me think about it and get back to you," is a perfectly acceptable response in the meantime. Just be sure to really do that; don't ignore the problem. Change into your uncomfortable pants, think about the issues, decide where your boundary lines fall for this situation, weigh options, and go from there.

Better Bitch Brunch

Not everyone will be a jerk about your boundaries. In fact, some might fall into the "encouraging influencer" category. Meaning, they fully support this change in you and offer supportive feedback and ideas.

These are the people that respond with things like

- Thank you for telling me.

- I didn't realize I was doing that; I'm sorry.

- Wanna grab a bottle of wine and talk about everything?

- Please point out the next time this happens.

- How can I help? What do you need from me?

- I'll pick you up at 10:00 a.m. on Saturday for brunch.

These are also the people who have watched and listened to your struggles, been there for heart-to-hearts, and probably know lots of your dirty secrets (because they are probably the same as theirs). If you have these people in your life, celebrate these relationships.

Your time and energy are well spent on people with whom you can laugh and cry, be vulnerable, confess fears, and share dreams—including the weird ones.

If you don't have these people, taking the steps to embrace your authentic self will naturally shift your circle; you will find your people.

Chapter 12:

Boss Bitch

Your boss bitch already exists and is screaming from the rooftops to let her out! But what that really means is you are already enough; you already have the tools you need to embrace who you are and live unapologetically. We have the right to be our own bitch and communicate our needs, to be sensitive, bold, mad, sad, blunt, or soft. Finding your inner boss bitch is inevitably about finding yourself.

Bitch, Please

Look, I realize this was a lot to digest, and it's easy to feel overwhelmed. We're definitely trying to become *less* stressed and anxious; doing this type of work can feel just like adding another log on the fire when you've already got quite the blaze sucking all the air from the room.

Just take a breath. You might have read this book in one or two sittings, but what I'm asking you to do will take time. Nothing in here is meant to be presented simplistically or suggest that this isn't a very hard process. Be brave—you've got this!

When we're scared of something but do it anyway, we flex our bravery muscle, and it then gets increasingly easier the more we do so. The fear doesn't necessarily go away, but you've proven to yourself that although it's there, lurking in the background, you can do it anyway.

Human beings are clearly creatures of habit, but that doesn't need to be restricted to negative or unhealthy habits. When you can name your fears, look them—and yourself—in the face and say, "Buckle up, Bitch. We're doing this anyway," you signal to your brain that you're taking the reins and are no longer just along for the ride.

There is a huge reward spike to our mental and emotional health when we're brave. But being brave isn't always visible; it isn't always loud and in your face. Sometimes being brave means turning the page or answering questions honestly; it means sticking up for yourself in quiet, but consistent, ways. Being brave can just be whispering out loud to yourself that you need some help.

You don't need to force yourself to do anything that feels like it's "too much;" you're the one who has to make that distinction. Sometimes being brave is making that phone call or googling where to find the resources you need for professional help and support from a doctor or therapist. There are so many options available that make it an incredibly low barrier to reach out to someone. I'm not saying it's easy mentally and emotionally, but help is really only a click away.

I'd Like a Venti, Iced, Sugar-Free, Pumpkin Spice Latte With Oak Milk

We're complicated beings with complicated lives. For your coffee, maybe it's a bit much, but for your life, it's actually pretty wonderful. The sections in this book are meant to meld together to provide holistic support for embracing and cultivating your boss bitch mentality.

For example, you wouldn't just want to create boundaries without examining your fears; you wouldn't just examine your fears and then stuff them back under the bed. It's not easy. There are a lot of moving parts, and the problem is exacerbated by prolonged refusal and rejection of self.

If you're struggling with where to start, go with "The Easy Stuff." Not only are those questions fun, but they're also a great way to warm up your brain to prime it for further deep thought. You can even go through them a couple times to see if you come up with different answers. It would also be fun to do with a trusted friend.

Just take everything in a serving size that works best for you in your unique situation. If you have pain points coming in from all directions, you can either tackle the big thing first or start with the smallest item. Either way, small steps add up to big changes and even just a little relief will go a long way.

The message is just to do something: change one thing, talk with one person openly and honestly, answer one of the hard questions, set one boundary, do one brave thing. You've already read this book and that goes on the list!

I'm Too Hungover

By the end here, you've probably gone through a bit of emotional baggage; maybe even some stuff you thought was lost to the airport forever. You're probably at a stage in your life where you know exactly how to cure your own hangover—time to make those skills work for you in other departments!

Grab your journal, take a few minutes to think about how you're feeling now, and write it down.

That can be a variety of entry types:

- You can create a list with just single words that represent feelings (excited, nervous, confused, etc.).

- You can write a letter to yourself right now expressing your thoughts.

- You can write a letter, forgiving yourself for anything you may have been holding onto concerning blame or regret.

- You can write a letter to your future self, expressing your goals, desires, dreams, and any promises you want to make.

- You can jot down what you took away from this experience and what you plan to do from here.

- You can create a plan with all the small steps outlined and detailed to get you started.

- If you are more artistically inclined, you can just sketch or doodle images that correspond to your feelings.

- You can make a list of people who you know truly support you and your efforts.

After you've taken a moment for one (or all) of the above, think about the following:

- What stood out to you the most while going through any of the chapters or exercises?

- What's the first thing you want to work on?

- Who's the first person you want to share everything with? (Then reach out and do just that.)

Pop Quiz: Who's Your Bitch?

Answer: You. You're your bitch. Yes, we've spent a bunch of time on what other people are doing in *relation* to you, but it's ultimately about *you*, specifically, and embracing who you are.

What does that mean? Envision yourself giving a hug to your inner woman, your deep-rooted femininity and by that, I mean the characteristics that traits for anyone who identifies as feminine or a woman. This typically means compassion, kindness, thoughtfulness, generosity, nurturing, sympathy, empathy, creativity, understanding, and supportiveness—basically all things you are with other people in mind.

Share those beautiful traits and characteristics with yourself! Embrace your desires and goals. Give the person inside of you a voice and then actively listen to her.

Our inner boss bitch is about power over ourselves not control being pressed in from the outside. If you want, another fun exercise to do is to create a personalized B.I.T.C.H. acronym. This can help you feel empowered with this word rather than discouraged or shamed.

You will use each letter in the word bitch to construct a statement that belongs to you. I have a few examples if you'd like to use one of these or create one that is uniquely you:

- Blazing Intense Tenacious Caring Heart

- Beautiful Inside Through Constant Healing

- Believe Inner Truth Conquers Hate

- Bodacious Individual Taking Control Herself

Boss Bitch Club

What does it mean to be part of the boss bitch club? Who are boss bitches? These are not just a stereotypical ballbuster wearing a power suit and Louis Vuitton's; I mean, that totally works too, but we're so much more:

- We speak what's in our hearts.

- We stand up for our friends.

- We don't take shit from anyone.

- When we say, "No," we mean, "Fuck, no."

- We're analytical, passionate, and understanding.

- We're our own heroes.

- We know what's in our hearts and try to live authentically.

- When we fail, we dust that shit off as much as possible, and get back up.

- We laugh, cry, sing, and shout.

- We're brave and move forward regardless of also being afraid.

- We're individuals, mothers, daughters, sisters, friends, partners, aunts, and grandmas.

- We have passion projects.

This list really could go on forever so feel free to add to it to fully see and realize yourself as part of the boss bitch club. This book is one of my passion projects because I want everyone to see themselves somewhere on this list and live outside of where they may have felt confined. I'm passionate about sharing what I've learned with anyone who needs the extra little push or reminder of what a strong, confident woman they already are.

Conclusion

Almost 20 years ago, I thought life was perfect: I was in love and pregnant with baby number one. I had to quit school, start working, and plan a life for my baby, me, and my "forever" person. I was dreaming. Some of you may have had that dream come true, and if you are one of the lucky ones, you are blessed.

You never really see sometimes until there is a little one in your arms, and all the shit you used to ignore becomes a reality. For instance, the fact that the man you love will never grow up (some never do), your priorities are not aligned, and you realize you're playing the game of life without knowing any of the rules—you've been chasing a dream that wasn't possible.

I never realized the damage (mentally) he created for me. As I slowly stepped away from the relationship, I backslid in a moment of weakness, and created baby number two. Yep, oh boy, two boys in fact, 19 months apart; a toddler and an infant looking to me for everything, and I looked up and realized I didn't have my person. I didn't have someone to support and care for me or to help with these little precious bundles.

I was fed up, done with his ass, and that was okay. I realized just how much my family really does love me—the good, bad, and ugly. They were an amazing support system; not only for me, but also for my children. It took a few years, but I feel like I was able to put the pieces together into the actual shape of me.

Our inner boss bitch can be good, ugly, naïve, passionate, and frustratingly honest. She's capable of badassery beyond measure; the one that tells us in the back of our minds when we know we are right and everything inside of us is screaming from behind bars to SAY IT, be THAT BITCH, and stand up for yourself. And, if necessary, realize you may have stuck your foot in your mouth with an "oops" moment and apologize—thoughtfully and genuinely.

You have to be brave and let your "mini monster" take the stage sometimes to speak up for yourself, feeling good in the process.

I always think back to when I was pregnant with my oldest child; the situation I was in was not ideal, but LOVE can be so damn blinding. At the time, I had not yet found my voice and all of the "what ifs" in life were becoming an increasing, debilitating pressure.

It was almost as if a light bulb burst inside of me as I dug deep from within and finally stood up—spoke up—and said, "You know what? I can DO this all by myself!" I found my mini monster that had been hiding, that took me *years* to find, and that bitch saved me.

That part of me sparked a drive and passion to want more for me, the child I was carrying, and the WOMAN I knew I *could* be! That heartache was incredibly painful; after realizing the beautiful world in front of me and the future brewing on the horizon, I spent the subsequent year and a half "fixing" me. I recognized that straddling the divide between who I wanted to be and who I was presently embodying was a constant back and forth that wasn't doing me any favors—it was actually incredibly harmful.

I really reflected and grew. My mini monster turned out to be my personal warrior and voice of reason, and I've spent considerable, quality time nurturing and defining that relationship, growing it into one of trust.

That's exactly what I want for you; it's what I want for everyone. Give yourself permission to try, but also to get it wrong—all of it: life, the goals you set from this book, making dinner, you name it. We can't stop everything from going to shit once and a while, but we can develop our inner strength—our boss bitch—so she shows up for us when we need her the most.

References

Anthony, K. (2017, July 22). *The five real reasons you keep losing your shit on your kids*. Your Divorce Survival Guide. https://kateanthony.com/the-five-real-reasons-you-keep-losing-your-shit-on-your-kids/

Babauta, L. (2022, May 1). *A guide to beating the fears that are holding you back*. Zen Habits. https://zenhabits.net/a-guide-to-beating-the-fears-that-are-holding-you-back/

Borbala. (2020, August 19). *15 questions to identify your FEARS*. Follow Your Own Rhythm. https://www.followyourownrhythm.com/blog-1/2018/10/15/how-to-identify-your-fears-15-insightful-questions

Brooks, M. (1997). Bitch [Song]. On *Blurring the edges* [Album]. Capitol Records.

Brooten-Brooks, M. C. (2022, January 24). *What is boundary setting? A guide to setting limits with parents, partners, friends, and co-workers*. Verywell Health. https://www.verywellhealth.com/setting-boundaries-5208802

Chesak, J. (2018, December 10). *The no BS guide to protecting your emotional space.* Healthline. https://www.healthline.com/health/mental-health/set-boundaries#learn-other-peoples-boundaries-too

Corleone, J. (2022, April 20). *How your body shape changes with age.* VeryWell Fit. https://www.verywellfit.com/how-your-body-shape-changes-with-age-2223440

Devine, M. (2017). *It's ok that you're not ok: Meeting grief and loss in a culture that doesn't understand.* Sounds True.

Fernandez, C. (2018, November 21). *10 celebrities on the importance of setting boundaries.* Oprah Daily. https://www.oprahdaily.com/life/relationships-love/g23323893/celebrity-setting-boundaries-quotes/?slide=7

4 surprising things that happen to women. (2017, May 30). DailyHealthWire. https://www.trihealth.com/dailyhealthwire/living-well/womens-health/4-surprising-things-that-happen-to-women

Fox, V. (2015, January 23). *50 inspiring quotes from fearless women.* Bentley University. https://www.bentley.edu/news/50-quotes-from-fearless-women

Girlboss. (2019, May 20). *7 ways fear is holding you back (and how to overcome it)*. Girlboss. https://girlboss.com/blogs/read/ruth-soukup-do-it-scared

Hailey, L. (2022, May 11). *How to set boundaries: 5 ways to draw the line politely.* Science of People. https://www.scienceofpeople.com/how-to-set-boundaries/

Henson, J. (Director). (1986). *Labyrinth* [Film]. Henson Associates, Inc.

Identifying fears. (2020, June 19). Hoffman. https://www.hoffmaninstitute.org/identifying-fears/

James, M. (2015, May 17). *6 signs that fear is holding you back.* Psychology Today. https://www.psychologytoday.com/us/blog/focus-forgiveness/201505/6-signs-fear-is-holding-you-back

Klienman, S., Ezzell, M., & Frost, A. C. (2009). Reclaiming critical analysis: The social harms of "bitch". *Sociological Analysis,* 3(1), 47-68. https://www.jmu.edu/socanth/sociology/wm_library/ezzell.reclaiming_critical_analysis.pdf

Merriam-Webster. (n.d.). Bitch. In *Merriam-Webster.com dictionary.* https://www.merriam-webster.com/dictionary/bitch

Morel, P. (Director). (2008). *Taken* [Film]. EuropaCorp.

Newman, T. (2021, October 30). *Dissecting terror: How does fear work?* MedicalNewsToday. https://www.medicalnewstoday.com/articles/323492#Why-do-we-freeze-when-we-are-scared?

Northwestern Medicine. (2020). *5 things you never knew about fear.* Northwestern Medicine. https://www.nm.org/healthbeat/healthy-tips/emotional-health/5-things-you-never-knew-about-fear

Oprah Winfrey quotes. (n.d.). Brainy Quote. https://www.brainyquote.com/authors/oprah-winfrey-quotes

Raypole, C. (2020, February 26). *A (realistic) guide to becoming self-actualized.* Healthline. https://www.healthline.com/health/self-actualization#characteristics

Robertson, C. (2016, March 11). *The science behind guilt— and why it is never the answer.* Medium. https://medium.com/@Willpowered/the-science-behind-guilt-and-why-it-is-never-the-answer-2dd986213882

Selva, J. (2018, January 5). *How to set healthy boundaries: 10 examples + PDF worksheets.* PositiviePsychology.com. https://positivepsychology.com/great-self-care-setting-healthy-boundaries/

Snyder, B. (2017, May 19). *The 10 biggest fears holding you back from success.* CNBC. https://www.cnbc.com/2017/05/18/the-10-biggest-fears-holding-you-back-from-success.html

Sowers, M., Zheng, H., Tomey, K., Karvonen-Gutierrez, C., Jannausch, M., Li, X., Yosef, M., & Symons, J. (2007). Changes in body composition in women over six years at midlife: Ovarian and chronological aging. *The Journal of Clinical Endocrinology & Metabolism*, 92(3), 895-901. https://academic.oup.com/jcem/article/92/3/895/2597229?login=false

Whedon, J. (Director). (2012). *The Avengers* [Film]. Marvel Studios.

White, E. (2022, May 23). *6 signs your fear is holding you captive.* Women On Top. https://www.womenontopp.com/6-signs-your-fear-is-holding-you-captive/

A woman's changing body. (2021, August 14). Well Stated By Canyon Ranch. https://www.canyonranch.com/well-stated/post/a-womans-changing-body/

Zahrai, S. (2020, January 27). *The four-letter word holding women back at work—And how to overcome it.* Forbes. https://www.forbes.com/sites/forbescoachesc

ouncil/2020/01/27/the-four-letter-word-holding-women-back-at-work-and-how-to-overcome-it/?sh=54b45d061302

www.ingramcontent.com/pod-product-compliance
Lightning Source LLC
LaVergne TN
LVHW020930090426
835512LV00020B/3302